WESTERN REGION STEAM
1950–1965

'43XX' Class 2-6-0 No. 6390 on Hatton Bank with a Class 'F' freight which included many wooden bodied wagons. This was a one-off visit to Hatton made by Norman Lockett and other photographs taken on this occasion are included within these pages. *15th October 1952*
No. 6390 dated from 1921, one of only 35 of these numerous 'Moguls' built for the GWR by Robert Stephenson & Co. At the time of Norman's photograph, the locomotive was allocated to Banbury (84C) but was about to be transferred to St. Phillip's Marsh (82B), a move recorded as taking place during the three-week period ending 1st November 1952.

On one of those halcyon early summer days, the likes of which those who are of an age to remember holidays during the 1950s tend to reminisce about, Norman Lockett has positioned himself against the stone parapet wall at the Teignmouth end of Shaldon Bridge. It is low water in the Teign Estuary, as No. 6022 *King Edward III* accelerates away from its passage through Teignmouth with the westbound 'Cornish Riviera Express', comprising thirteen coaches in the then standard crimson lake & cream livery. *Saturday, 25th June 1955*

Rather remarkably, there does not appear to be a soul in sight on such a sunny day – not even any children in the lineside playground! Also, it is surprising that there does not seem to be any BR Mk1 coaches in the formation of this train, although there may be some lurking towards the rear. The first four coaches appear to be Hawksworth designs. Then follow two Collett large window types and what appears to be the Restaurant car (Kitchen/First). The coach in front of it may well be an SO used for meals. The following three coaches again look like Hawksworth designs. It is likely, therefore, that the formation comprised ten coaches for St. Ives (taken on from St. Erth by a pair of '45xx' 2-6-2Ts), followed by the Penzance portion (of three coaches). The summer time table for 1955 was supposed to have commenced on 13th June. However, the ASLEF national rail strike resulted in the railway time table for the summer season being put back officially to commence from Monday 27th June, two days after Norman Lockett took this photograph.

WESTERN REGION STEAM
1950-1965

MIKE ARLETT & DAVID LOCKETT

Lightmoor Press

Collett 0-6-0 No. 2218 passes the site of Wilton North station (note the overgrown platform), heading in the direction of Salisbury with what Norman Lockett described as 'a banana train'. Messrs Geest Bananas owned a depot at Warminster used to ripen the fruit, so it is probable that the branded vans towards the rear of this formation were conveying bananas to various wholesalers. *21st March 1964*

No. 2218 had been allocated to Westbury and records show it reallocated to Templecombe (ex-S&D) during the week ending 21/3/64. Note the date of Norman's photograph; it is pure speculation but was this train the means used to transfer the 0-6-0 from Westbury (via Salisbury) to Templecombe? Both the front numberplate and shedplate have been removed, the number having been chalked on the buffer beam. No. 2218 was withdrawn from Templecombe on 13/11/64. Wilton (former) GWR station, had been renamed Wilton North by BR in 1949 and the nearby SR station renamed Wilton South. Along with all other intermediate stations on the ex-GWR route from Warminster to Salisbury, Wilton North was closed to passenger services on 19th September 1955.

FRONT COVER PICTURE: Having just taken over the train, No. 5017 *The Gloucestershire Regiment 28th 61st* **sets off from Gloucester (Central) with the 2.40pm semi-fast to Swindon, a service which started from Cheltenham (St. James) at 2.10pm.** *3rd October 1955*

REAR COVER PICTURE: Collett 0-4-2T No. 1472 pulls away from Cirencester (Town) for the 4¼ mile run to the junction with the main line at Kemble. This train was a last day special organised by the Gloucestershire Railway Society. *Sunday, 5th April 1964*

NOTE: In many instances throughout this book – thanks to information kindly provided by the *The HSBT Project* – references are made to the dates when a locomotive was recorded 'in' and 'out' of (or 'to' and 'from') Swindon Works for an overhaul. In this context, 'in' or 'to' was the date available to the Works and 'out' or 'from' was when the engine was handed back to the R&M, who would test it and run it in before it went back to home shed diagrams. Where used as an abbreviation, 'w/e' means 'week ending'. For example, a locomotive transferred during the period 4w/e 11/6/55 means it was transferred during the four week period ending 11/6/1955.

Previously published in the Norman Lockett Archive:
The Somerset & Dorset Railway 1935-1966, Mike Arlett & David Lockett, 2009, 2nd ed. 2010
Great Western Steam 1935-1949, Mike Arlett & David Lockett 2010

CONTENTS

Published by LIGHTMOOR PRESS

© Lightmoor Press, Mike Arlett & David Lockett 2011

Designed by Mike Arlett & Neil Parkhouse

British Library Cataloguing-in-Publication Data. A catalogue record for this book is available from the British Library

ISBN: 9781899889 60 0

LIGHTMOOR PRESS

Unit 144B, Lydney Trading Estate, Harbour Road, Lydney, Gloucestershire GL15 5EJ

www.lightmoor.co.uk

Lightmoor Press is an imprint of Black Dwarf Lightmoor Publications Ltd

Printed & bound by TJ International, Padstow, Cornwall

FOREWORD

In *Great Western Steam 1934-1949*, we presented a selection of more than 170 photographs taken by Norman Lockett and featuring motive power of what was his favourite railway company. We decided the period covered in that volume should extend beyond the date of Nationalisation (1st January 1948) to include the following two years because – other than some experimental liveries – outwardly there was, at first, little to suggest to the casual observer the many changes that were afoot. F.W. Hawksworth, the last of the GWR Chief Mechanical Engineers, remained in post until his retirement at the end of 1949 and during those first two years of the newly created Western Region of British Railways, production of several GWR types of motive power was allowed to continue. Indeed, the construction of 'Castles', 'Halls' and a further batch of 'Manors' continued into 1950, and whilst these proved to be the last tender-type designs from the pre-nationalised era, a considerable number of GWR-inspired tank engines (many of which proved to be superfluous to requirements) were built, mainly by private sector constructors, until 1956.

In this book we present just over 240 more photographs from 'The Norman Lockett Archive'. The first thing to note is that, overall, there is a wider geographical spread of lineside locations photographed by Norman than it was possible to present in *GWR Steam 1934-1949*. As we have pointed out before, Norman relied on public transport in pursuit of his lineside photography and this, together with the limited hours he was able to devote to his hobby, restricted considerably the range of different locations he was able to visit. However, in 1956 he met Ivo Peters, who shared his passion for railway photography and whose home was in Bath, the city to which Norman moved to work and to live from September 1957. The two photographers struck up a lasting friendship and often travelled together in Ivo's Bentley, visiting locations far and wide. Many of these were to areas beyond the boundaries of the Western Region and, hence, to locations not appropriate to this book. As the number of hours worked each week started to be relaxed from the late-1950s, Norman was able to spend a little more time in pursuit of his hobby although, as David recalls, his father had other interests, including gardening and the Somerset County Cricket Club, of which he was an ardent supporter.

By adopting the title *Western Region Steam 1950-1965*, we feel we can reasonably include any locomotive Norman photographed running (or in some cases just standing) on Western Region metals; hence, our excuse for sneaking in just the occasional 'foreigner'! In addition, examples of some of the BR 'Standard' classes of engines are featured. As with our previous two books published by Lightmoor Press, we have attempted to ensure that this new publication contains only a few of Norman Lockett's photographs which have appeared previously in print. From the 1950s, Norman, by then a member of the Railway Photographic Society, started to submit the occasional photograph to *Trains Illustrated*, the editor of which publication was quick to recognise the quality of the results of his skills with a quarter-plate camera. In the knowledge that Norman often accompanied Ivo Peters to the lineside, we have also endeavoured to exclude many photographs which, effectively, would be replications of those previously published by Ivo.

However, from 1959, when Ivo purchased his first cine camera, it was often the case that, whilst Norman took a photograph, Ivo might film the same scene. For those readers who have access to the videos marketed as *The Ivo Peters Collection*, you may notice how often Norman can be seen taking a photograph. Now look through the pages of this book to see some of the images Norman captured on such occasions!

A previously published picture has been reused if it happens to be the only (or a rare) occasion when Norman photographed at a specific location or featured an example of a class of locomotive for what proved to be the last occasion. Otherwise, as before, our only justification for republishing a photograph is because of the great technological advances made in more recent times, enabling scans to be made directly from Norman's original glass plate negatives rather than from his own prints. Again, we are retaining the same format and style as per our earlier books, including a considerable number of full page pictures and a few spread across two pages, so please accept our by now customary apologies for the amount of 'book turning' that will be required. Generally speaking, we have also continued on a time-related theme, to take you through from 1950 to 1965. Just occasionally, where it is logical to do so, we have included a photograph from one period into another, in order that photographs featuring the same 'locale' can be brought together. As such, the pictures are not necessarily in strict 'date order'. As already mentioned, in one respect this book differs from the earlier GWR volume for, as the years progressed, a wider range of locations can be featured. To be honest, there is just one exception – the sea wall section around Teignmouth! For this, Mike accepts full responsibility, because the picturesque seaside town of Teignmouth remains – to this day – a personal favourite. In any case, Norman's photographs along this famous stretch of the main line are sufficient in number to fill very many pages of a book! Furthermore, it is the town where the two compilers of this book first came 'face to face' 25 years ago.

If you have thumbed your way through our earlier books you will be aware of the cameras and other equipment used by Norman, and his contemporary approach to photography as influenced by the 'three-quarters front' exponents who led the field in the 1920s and '30s. We do not intend to repeat all those details here – so if you are interested, we refer you back to our two previous volumes featuring 'The Norman Lockett Archive'. In any case, when looking at those many hundreds of glass plate negatives dating from 1950 and subsequent years, it is evident that whilst Norman never abandoned his preferred 'three-quarter front' format, on an increasing number of occasions he included the wider and, we think, more interesting vista.

Our thanks again to our publishing team led by Neil Parkhouse; it really is so beneficial to work with publishers who are very much enthusiasts at heart. Finally, to our wives Sandra and Daphne, our thanks for having put up with the very many hours we have spent scanning, assembling, researching and captioning this further selection of evocative photographs from 'The Norman Lockett Archive'. We hope you will enjoy the result. Our acknowledgements follow.

Mike Arlett & David Lockett, 2011

ACKNOWLEDGEMENTS

We wish to thank David's brother Geoff and his sister Norma, to whom David has turned to confirm (or sometimes contradict!) his recollections of when (for example) their father made his career move and relocation to Bath.

John Lewis, the authority on GWR coaching stock, has again provided Mike with much detailed information, for which we wish to record our most grateful thanks. Our thanks also to Chris Osment, who has clarified and confirmed for Mike various questions regarding signalling at several of the locations featured within this book. Invaluable help has also been provided by Brian Macdermott, who has responded to the queries from Mike which has necessitated access to WR Working Time tables.

As was the case with our earlier titles, we wish to acknowledge Mike's use of the *Railway Observer*, the house magazine of the Railway Correspondence & Travel Society, the HSBT Project (see page 182), *The Railway Magazine*, *Trains Illustrated* and *Railway World*. Should there be any errors that have crept in regarding locomotive allocations, repairs, dates and the like, these – we are confident – will be down to Mike and his derisory keyboard skills (typing errors!) rather than those who have provided information to him.

As with our first volume *Great Western Steam 1934-1949*, Mike wishes to acknowledge the information gained from the two-part monograph penned by O.S. Nock entitled *The GWR Stars, Castles & Kings,* published by David & Charles. Much more recently (2009), Irwell Press Ltd published *The Book of the Castle 4-6-0s* by Ian Sixsmith, which provides a detailed record of every member of this famous class of locomotive. Richard Derry is thanked for help with information regarding the 'Britannia' Class locomotives. Thanks also to Richard Croucher, Chairman of the Great Western Society and to the Saltash Heritage Museum & Local History Centre. Invaluable help has also been provided by Brian Macdermott, who has responded to queries from Mike necessitating access to WR Working Time tables.

A book entitled *The Ringing Grooves of Change* was consulted for several historical facts concerning the GWR in and around Bath. Written by Andrew Swift and published by Akeman Press, it is a title which may have escaped the attention of many a railway historian. The sub title, *Brunel & The Coming Of The Railway To Bath*, might give a better indication as to the content of this very interesting book.

An omission from our previous two books in this series we must put to rights is the printer and binder, TJ International of Padstow, Cornwall. They really have done us proud thus far with the efforts taken to achieve such a high quality of reproduction from what, even for this book – which depicts a later period of steam railway photography – comprises glass plate negatives which (in 2011) are between 46 and 61 years old.

Except where noted otherwise, all text and captioning has been prepared by Mike who, as before, makes no claims as to originality of information other, perhaps, than in relation to some of the asides, which it is hoped might add a little to your enjoyment of the book. In most cases, information is based on notes made by the photographer.

Norman Lockett, second from right, flanked by Mr Stratford, Chief Guide (left) and Mr Cooper, Assistant Guide (holding the Works cat!), pose for Ivo Peters in front of No. 7029 *Clun Castle*. This was during a visit of the Bath Railway Society to Swindon Works on 8th November 1959. Also present in this view are Ken Padfield (far left) and Ron Hurst, the latter being the founder and, for several early years, Secretary of the Bath Railway Society. With a Heavy General overhaul almost completed, No. 7029 had just been provided with a twin blastpipe and double chimney, and a 4-row superheater. Notice the number of the newly-fitted boiler, No. 7664, chalked on the bottom of the rim of the smokebox.

From a photograph by Ivo Peters, courtesy Julian Peters

Viewed from the south side of the Loop Line serving Weston-super-Mare, 'Castle' Class No. 5062 *Earl of Shaftesbury* nears its destination with 'The Merchant Venturer', one of five new titled trains (this, the only example on the WR) which BR introduced to run from the late spring of 1951 to celebrate the Festival of Britain. Each of the new trains was to be formed of the first of the new BR standard corridor coaching stock and dining cars. Taunton-based No. 5062 will have taken over at Temple Meads to complete the run to Weston. The fireman and at least one passenger appear to have noticed Norman at the lineside with his quarter plate camera! *14th May 1951*

The inaugural service of 'The Merchant Venturer', the 11.15am Paddington-WSM and 4.35pm return, ran on 3rd May 1951, the first of two days of celebrations marking the opening of the Festival of Britain Exhibition on the South Bank of the River Thames. Locomotives were changed at Temple Meads in both directions. On the first day, No. 5062 had taken over from No. 7025 Sudeley Castle, which had brought the train down from Paddington.

SECTION 1
1950-1954

At the start of the 1950s, Norman was living in Weston-super-Mare, the town where he was born and to which his family had returned from Plymouth during the war years. From Weston, he travelled by train and bus to and from work in Bristol, where he was employed as the manager of the Southmead branch of Boots the Chemist, about 3 miles north of the city centre.

In *Great Western Steam 1935-1949*, we featured some of Norman's many photographs taken around the area of his home town. He continued to visit the lineside thereabouts into the 1950s but we have made the decision to exclude – to the greater part – further examples of photographs taken at any of the same locations as featured in the earlier book. Other than just a few photographs, which serve as the 'continuity link' between the previous book and this album, any later examples are usually pictures which depict something new or unusual in terms of motive power or rolling stock. Otherwise, where we have included a lineside location at or near Weston-super-Mare, it will be from a camera position different to that featured in the earlier volume. However, during

the early years of the 'Fifties', Norman started to visit some new locations in addition to those traditional lineside haunts nearer his home town.

From 2nd April 1950, the Railway Executive implemented adjustments to the boundaries of the six Regions of BR as created on Nationalisation just two years earlier. Within the area covered in this book, the WR gained responsibility of the former LM&SR lines south of Selly Oak to Bristol and Bath, including branch lines. Conversely, all the WR lines south of the route of the Reading-Westbury-Taunton main line were transferred to the SR. The WR also gained control of the Somerset & Dorset north of Cole, including the branch lines (for which see our first title in this series, *The Somerset & Dorset Railway 1935-1966*). However, in most cases, the operating arrangements for these lines were retained by the Region formally responsible. So, whilst some of the stations and other structures along these routes were destined to be repainted in the house colours of the new 'owners', the motive power remained very much the same as before.

Designed by F.W. Hawksworth, 0-6-0PT No. 8413 was built by W.G. Bagnall Ltd and delivered to Swindon, where it arrived on 11th January 1950. After those at Swindon were satisfied with the builder's work and had fitted ATC gear, the engine was put into traffic on 23rd January, allocated to St. Philip's Marsh (82B). Norman's photograph, taken at 7.20pm on a Wednesday evening, shows No. 8413 heading along the loop from Worle Junction towards Weston-super-Mare with a Class 'F' freight train, which comprises a very mixed consignment including, at the rear, several wagons loaded with timber. *26th July 1950*
No. 8413 remained based at St. Philip's Marsh until transferred to Southall on 4th January 1957 (during the period from 8/9/56 to 4/1/57 it was recorded as 'stored'). Withdrawn on 10th January 1961, the 0-6-0 was cut up at Stafford Road Works, Wolverhampton, the date recorded as 24th February 1961.

HOME TOWN TERRITORY

Allocated new to Bristol Bath Road, 4-6-0 'County' Class No. 1007 *County of Brecknock* **hurries along the main line, just beyond Worle Junction, with the 12.35pm Manchester (London Road) to Plymouth, which also conveyed a portion to Kingswear. The leading coach is ex-LM&SR, probably a Brake Compo. Luckily, the prevailing wind was blowing off the Bristol Channel sweeping away an exhaust which suggests some indifferent coal or poor combustion.** *16th July 1952*

When photographing traffic on the main line between Worle and Uphill, Norman rarely took up a lineside position this close to Worle Junction, generally preferring locations a little farther to the south west. The signal box controlling the junction can just be made out, being 530 yards north east of the Down Starting signal seen here in the foreground. Frederick Hawksworth's two-cylinder 'County' Class was introduced in 1945. No. 1007 did not receive nameplates until January 1948. Unlike No. 1000, which entered traffic with a double blastpipe and chimney, No. 1007 was built with a single blastpipe and chimney which had become the standard for all other members of the class until, between 1956-59, all were fitted with a different design of double chimney. This three-quarter view shows well the space between the splasher and the separately mounted nameplate necessary on this side of these engines to provide clearance for the reversing rod. On the opposite side, the nameplate was fixed to the top of the splasher.

OPPOSITE PAGE TOP: Norman has positioned himself on the Down side of the main line between the junctions at Worle and Uphill to photograph 'Mogul' No. 9309 with a westbound Class 'F' freight. Something has attracted the attention of the fireman, who has called his driver to the near side of the cab. This is a location which features heavily in our GWR book but these low angle shots by Norman were fairly uncommon. *12th August 1951*
Built during Collett's regime at Swindon, the '93XX' locomotives were effectively an updated version of the '43XX' mixed traffic class. Dating from early 1932, this final series, like some similarly modified engines earlier in the series, carried a heavy casting fixed behind the front buffer beam which restricted their use to 'red' routes, under the former GWR system of classification for routing purposes. They were later modified by the removal of this feature during the latter half of the 1950s. The resultant reduction in weight enabled these 2-6-0s to be reclassified as 'blue' route engines, whereupon they were renumbered into the '73XX' series. One end of the casting is clearly visible in this photograph.

OPPOSITE PAGE BOTTOM: Transferred from Stafford Road to Bristol (82B – St. Philip's Marsh) during the period 4w/e 16th July 1949, No. 5919 *Worsley Hall* **heads southwards towards Highbridge with a lengthy Class 'F' freight. The locomotive looks in desperate need of a clean but – other than 'top link' motive power – this was not considered a priority by the beginning of the 1950s, especially at those depots which might have been suffering labour shortages to undertake such tasks. In fact, taking off one's 'rose-tinted glasses', such standards were not unknown even before the start of the Second World War. Notice that Brent Knoll can just be seen through the gap in the hedge on the far side of the line. This prominent land feature rises to a height of 449 feet above sea level.** *12th October 1950*
This is the only photograph taken by Norman which features the WR Main Line in the vicinity of Highbridge. He was visiting the town to photograph the S&D between Highbridge and Burnham-on-Sea (for which see our S&D volume in this series). Much more often, Norman could be found at the lineside just a few miles farther to the north around Brean Road but as that section of the main line featured heavily in the GWR volume, it is omitted here. The grey patches seen over the Up line are not a fault with the negative but appear to be the result of some spillage from a passing train. The covering of grime to No. 5919 makes those headlamp casings appear positively dazzling!

AROUND UPHILL JUNCTION

ABOVE: Sporting its BR lined black livery, No. 1014 *County of Glamorgan* regains speed from its call at Weston-super-Mare with 'The Devonian', the through Bradford to Kingswear service. *1st October 1953*
No. 1014 was withdrawn from Swindon on 24th April 1964. A project based at the Didcot HQ of the Great Western Society is in progress to recreate a 'new' No. 1014. This member of the class has been chosen to mark the contribution made by the Vale of Glamorgan Council and Woodham's Yard at Barry in providing 'donor' parts from other unrestored locomotives.

LEFT: No. 6833 *Calcot Grange* and No. 5924 *Dinton Hall* approach Weston-super-Mare having just passed onto the Loop Line at Uphill Junction. The main line runs behind the hedgerow seen level with the leading engine's buffer plank. The train is the 11.20am (Sundays) Penzance to Birmingham (Snow Hill) and Wolverhampton (Low Level). Through carriages were also carried from Paignton and Torquay. Norman recorded the time as 5.45pm, so the train was running about 10 minutes late, with a booked departure from Weston General station at 5.40pm. *26th July 1953*
The train has a five coach portion at the front and at least eight following. It is likely (as was certainly the case by 1956) that the front five coaches were those originating from Paignton, whilst the remainder (including a Dining car) formed the portion from Penzance. All would have been brought together at Newton Abbot.

The westbound 'Devonian' features again but here closer towards Uphill Junction. 'Castle' Class No. 5059 *Earl St Aldwyn* was one of the batch (No's 5043-63) which, in 1937, the GWR had decided should carry the names originally allocated to the '32XX' Class 4-4-0s. *12th August 1953*
This location, no more than a mile from Weston-super-Mare General station and on the long sweeping curve by which the Loop Line approached the main line at Uphill Junction, was a favourite with Norman. In the 1950s it was still bordered by fields – just the sort of rural backdrop more usually preferred by him and with the advantage of being close to home. Here today, the now single line loop serving Weston passes through an area much developed as part of the expanding seaside town.

Turning to look in the opposite direction (southwards towards the junction), doubtless this sight came as something of a surprise to Norman. He recorded the time as 6.05pm, so this was most likely the 3.40pm Exeter-Taunton-Bristol Temple Meads stopping train. What Churchward 2-8-0 No. 4702, allocated to Old Oak Common, was doing in charge must remain a mystery. Perhaps it was a balancing or 'filling in' turn? *12th August 1953*
The stock appears to be a 'scratch' set! The leading vehicle is an ex-LM&SR Passenger Brake Van, the next a Stanier Period III coach, followed by a Collett (possibly bow-ended) coach, a Collett 70ft 'South Wales' (possibly Third Class), with either a Collett large window or even another ex-LM&SR coach bringing up the rear. No. 4702, built in 1922 and withdrawn in 1962, spent much of her existence allocated to Old Oak Common. Uphill Junction Signal Box lay just beyond the right hand margin as viewed here. The wagons seen in the distance beyond the rear of the train are standing in the refuge siding featured on the next page.

Norman was standing by the Up side at Uphill Junction here, close to the signal box, with the Loop Line curving away to the left and the main line heading into the distance towards Worle Junction. Class '28XX' 2-8-0 No. 2883 is easing this heavy westbound freight out of the Down Refuge Siding (note the ringed signal arm authorising exit from the siding). The footplate crew – I suspect – were hoping for a run down the main line without too many further interruptions of being 'put inside' a loop or 'set back' into another refuge siding to enable following traffic to pass. *15th August 1954*

Just look at the length of this freight, doubtless handled with ease by one of these most impressive 2-8-0s. Little wonder they were a favourite with Norman Lockett. Mind you, other than a few very short and almost imperceptible gradients, the track hereabouts was level for mile after mile. No. 2883 (here allocated to 86E) dated from 1919 and was the last to enter service until 1938, when construction recommenced with a modified design which included a new pattern cylinder block and the provision of outside steam pipes, features yet to be incorporated into No. 2883 as seen here. The single refuge siding at Uphill Junction, which could accommodate a maximum of 58 wagons plus engine and brake van, was taken out of use with the closure of the signal box during late January 1972. On busy Bank Holiday periods, especially during the early 1950s, it was not unknown for this (and just about every other local refuge siding) to be used temporarily to store coaching stock such was the extent of excursion traffic.

No. 7029 *Clun Castle* pulls away from the General station at Weston-super-Mare with the 8.45am Plymouth to Manchester. As was usually the case, Norman noted the time and this confirmed the train to be 'on schedule' with an 11.56am departure from Weston. No. 7029 had been in service for less than 2½ years when photographed here, being the second member of the final batch of this famous class to be built, during 1950, at Swindon. *8th October 1952*

Why Norman did not commence taking photographs from this viewpoint on the Drove Road overbridge until 1952 is unknown. However, once 'bitten', he obviously took a liking to the location as he returned time after time to capture the view, looking westwards, as here, and in the contrary direction from the opposite parapet of the bridge. The General station can be seen in the background, to the left beyond the signal box, whilst Locking Road terminus is to the right, here partially obscured by the exhaust from No. 7029. By the way, I never cease to be amazed by how much incidental detail is revealed when the scans of Norman's photographs are enlarged way beyond what is possible with smaller format negatives. Take, for example, the large building seen on the skyline above the rear of the straight rake of coaches behind No. 7029. You might be able just to determine some signage extending the full length of the eaves of the prominent building. With the image enlarged (350%!), this clearly reads as 'Lalonde Bros & Parham' which David was able to confirm as a well-known firm of auctioneers, valuers, estate agents and furniture removers.

EASTBOUND DEPARTURES FROM WESTON

ABOVE: The four platform faces which made up Locking Road station can be seen on the right, as Laira-based No. 6024 *King Edward I* sets off 'wrong line' with the 7.05am (Sundays) Plymouth-Paddington. Note the turntable to the extreme right of this scene. *4th October 1953*

Locking Road station was opened in 1914 to handle the growing excursion and other holiday traffic to the seaside town. Until the late 1950s, very large numbers of holidaymakers – whether visiting Weston just for the day or for the traditional 'week by the sea' – continued to arrive and depart by train. By the 1960s, this was no longer the case and Locking Road station was closed on 6th September 1964. Today, almost inevitably, the site is occupied by a supermarket and a coach/car park.

RIGHT: The 7.05am (Sundays) Plymouth-Paddington is featured again, this time making a more conventional departure behind No. 1000 *County of Middlesex*. *19th September 1954*

Under normal circumstances, I am sure that our publisher would baulk at three photographs of the same location appearing on facing pages but this is done with a purpose here, to show the changes brought about with the fitting of a replacement lever frame to the signal box. Note the different positions of the rodding runs in the photographs opposite and on this page, bottom. A replacement frame was fitted facing the opposite way to the existing. The photograph, above, shows the interim period with both sets of rodding visible, those to the left yet to be brought into use. Careful study also reveals changes to the smoke pipe from a repositioned signal box stove!

No. 5982 *Harrington Hall*, in charge of the 6.35pm Bristol to Weston-super-Mare local, has just passed Worle Junction (the signal box controlling the junction is again seen in the distance) and within a further mile will pause at Weston Milton Halt, the penultimate call before arrival at General station. *10th June 1953*

Even though this is a location which featured prominently in the previous volume, I selected this photograph because it represents an example of what was once a familiar sight – a working which included one or more milk tank wagons. The rake of 6-wheelers seen here were empties returning from West Ealing in London, first on the 10.55am Kensington to Swindon. There, they were transferred to the 4.07pm Swindon to Bristol stopping train which, at Temple Meads, formed the 6.35pm service to Weston. The stock remained at Weston overnight and formed the 9.00am stopping train to Bristol the following morning. At Puxton & Worle, the milk tanks were shunted into the siding which served the adjacent Somerset Creamery, built by the London Cooperative Society in the 1920s as a railhead for local milk producers. Loaded tankers were collected, each evening, by the Wellington-West Ealing milk train. The creamery closed during the 1960s but a recent check revealed the buildings are extant albeit apparently now used to repair commercial road vehicles. Back in the 1950s, Puxton & Worle station and the adjacent milk factory, located in an area known as St. Georges, were surrounded by countryside. Nowadays, this area forms the eastern boundary of the housing and other developments which extend from Weston-super-Mare all the way to the M5 motorway.

NEAR WORLE JUNCTION

The linesides near Worle Junction were a favourite with Norman Lockett. Just a short walk from his home, he could alternate between the Loop Line (which served Weston-super-Mare) and the original Main Line (which avoided the seaside town). On a sunny evening, natural lighting was superb for taking photographs of Down trains, with the setting sun highlighting the front of each train. Conversely, most of Norman's photographs which feature Up trains hereabouts (less than two miles east of Weston-Super-Mare General and Locking Road stations) were taken in the mornings at weekends, or when not at work.

Heading eastwards, on the approach to Worle Junction, No. 5999 *Wollaton Hall* has a clear road for the main line towards Bristol. The 4-6-0, creating an impressive trail of exhaust, was recorded by Norman as heading an excursion from Taunton to South Wales. Weston Milton Halt, where Norman caught his train to work in Bristol, was sited immediately beyond the overbridge seen in the distance. Opened on 3rd July 1933, the halt served what, at that time, was the eastern outskirts of Weston, extending along and adjacent to the Locking Road. *5th October 1952*

FLAX BOURTON

Bristol, Bath Road-based 'Castle' Class No. 5048 *Earl of Devon* **approaches Flax Bourton from the west with the 7.0am Paignton to Bristol train. Notice that the leading coach is one of the 'Centenary' stock.** *7th June 1954*

OPPOSITE PAGE TOP: Under a threatening sky, No. 5071 *Spitfire* has just passed through the station of Flax Bourton (the Up platform and footbridge barely visible to the rear of the train) with the 9.40am Taunton to Cardiff semi-fast. The public time table showed this train (or, perhaps, some part of it) as working through to Porthcawl. Norman took this and the following photograph from a footbridge which crosses high above the line. Notice the goods loop served from the Down main line, whilst the Up side of the cutting is smothered with moon daisies. *7th June 1954*

OPPOSITE PAGE BOTTOM: Turning to look in the opposite direction (but on a different occasion) finds No. 5058 *Earl of Clancarty* emerging from the 110 yard-long Flax Bourton Tunnel with the 4.15pm Paddington-Plymouth. The train also conveyed through carriages to Paignton. However, passengers travelling to Taunton, Exeter and Plymouth were advised to catch the 5.30pm from Paddington which, travelling via the 'Berks & Hants' line, would deliver them earlier to their destination. *19th July 1954*
The shadow seen in the bottom foreground is that of the footbridge as cast by a setting sun. The Down Loop Line seen in the previous photograph commenced immediately to the west of the footbridge, hence is not visible in this view.

'CORNISH RIVIERA' (VIA BRISTOL!)

ABOVE: On two consecutive Sundays, the 9th and 16th May 1954, the 'Cornish Riviera' was diverted from the usual route (by way of the Berks & Hants line) to run via Bristol. The diversions were necessary because of bridge renewal works in the Newbury area. Despite the weather being somewhat dull, Norman was on hand at Bristol to photograph both Up and Down services. This is the view from the bottom of Victoria Park as No. 6027 *King Richard I* heads the Down 'Riviera' west of Temple Meads, on the approach to Bedminster station. Norman recorded the time of taking his photograph as 1.15pm, so assuming the train departed from Paddington at its scheduled time of 10.30am, it had taken 2hrs 45mins thus far. *16th May 1954*
The large church (St. Luke, Bedminster) seen mid-distance to the extreme left of the view was demolished in 1970. Immediately to the right of the church, the upper part of the tower (with pinnacles) forming the frontage to Bristol, Temple Meads, can be seen on the skyline.

Table 3

TABLE 3

CORNISH RIVIERA EXPRESS
Refreshment Car Service

LONDON (Paddington), PLYMOUTH, TRURO
and PENZANCE

WEEK DAYS and SUNDAYS

	E a.m.	S a.m.	SUNS a.m.			E a.m.	S a.m.	SUNS. a.m.
London (Padd'ton) dep.	10A30	10A30	10A30	Penzance ... .. dep.		10A 0	10A 0	9A45
				St. Erth ... .. „		10A10	..	9A55
	p.m.		p.m.	Gwinear Road ... „		10A22	10A22	..
Plymouth (N. Rd.) arr	2 45	..	3 25	Truro ... . „		10 52	10 52	10 38
				Par ... . „		11 22	..	11 10
Par .. .. .. „	3 47	..	..					
		p.m.				p.m.	p.m.	p.m.
Truro .. .. .. „	4 18	4 28	5 0	Plymouth (N. Rd.) „		12A30	12 30	12A20
Gwinear Road .. „	4 48	..	..	Exeter (St. David's) „		..	..	1 50
St. Erth .. .. „	4 58	5 12	5 48	London (Padd'ton) arr.		4 45	5 20	5 30
Penzance .. .. „	5 10	5 25	6 0					

A—Seats can be reserved in advance on payment of a fee of 1s. 0d. per seat (see page 31).
E—Except Saturdays.   S—Saturdays only.

LEFT: Table 3 from the BR Western Region public time tables for the summer 1954 services. You will note that the timings for the 'Cornish Riviera Express' on Sundays were not – by any stretch of the imagination – very exhilarating, with 4hrs 55mins allowed between Paddington and Plymouth, and 5hrs 10 mins in the opposite direction. On Mondays to Fridays the schedule was 4hrs 15mins in both directions and it was the wish of Western Region senior management to accelerate the timings of the 'CRE' – from the summer 1955 time table – to 4hrs for the Down train and, (initially what was set at) 4hrs 10mins in the Up direction. This pronouncement heralded a series of dynamometer tests during the spring of 1955. These tests, in turn, were the precursor to the redesign and modification of each locomotive of the 'King' Class with a twin orifice blastpipe and double chimney, which transformed their performance for what would prove their final years on this service. The first of the class so provided was No. 6015 *King Richard III* (for which see page 69).

By 3.35pm, the weather had improved a little (note the light shadows), as No. 6012 *King Edward VI* with the Up 'Cornish Riviera' is routed through Temple Meads via a centre road between platforms 8 (left) and 10. Again, if maintaining its usual schedule, the train would have been booked to depart Exeter St. Davids (where a call was made by the Up 'Riviera' on Sundays only) at 1.50pm. *16th May 1954* This is one of several classic views taken by Norman at Temple Meads with trains arriving from the west around the sweeping curve under the Bath Road Bridge. In the left background, much of Bath Road motive power depot (shed code 82A) is temporarily hidden from view by the passage of the train. Perhaps this being a Sunday afternoon explains why so few 'locospotters' appear to be on hand to witness the rare spectacle of the passage of the 'Cornish Riviera' via this route.

FIRST SIGHTINGS OF THE 'BRITANNIA' CLASS

According to various records, BR 'Britannia' Class 4-6-2 No. 70020 *Mercury* was outshopped from Crewe and delivered to Swindon, arriving on or around 31st July 1951. Those at Swindon were poking around with it (acceptance trials, test runs and, possibly at this early stage, fitting ATC) before the 'Pacific' was allocated to Old Oak Common, where it is first recorded in October 1951. The new locomotive is just setting off from Platform 4 at Temple Meads at 4.44pm, in charge of the 1.18pm Paddington to Weston-super-Mare. Some records have this engine 'into traffic' and allocated to OOC (81A) on 31st July 1951. The date of Norman's photograph is Wednesday 22nd August 1951 and a shedplate is yet to be fitted to the front of the smokebox door.

I am not too confident that Norman would have approved the inclusion of this photograph, as he had marginally misjudged the framing (see bottom edge). However, this and the photograph opposite were his first recorded sightings of two of these new BR 'Britannia Pacifics', a class which proved somewhat controversial within some parts of the Western Region's Operating Department! My main purpose in using this picture is the sight of the young lads and their obvious excitement at seeing this brand new 'apparition' – perhaps for the first time. It is a photograph which brings back memories of such events to this writer. Notice the Temple Meads Loco Yard signal box in the right background.

Serendipity! In early September 2011, just days after my publisher emailed me computer files of the first batch of page layouts for this book, I was at Taunton station, where I had a wait of around an hour for my train. A good opportunity, I thought, to retire to the coffee shop on Platform 5 to read through and recheck (for the umpteenth time!) for any errors to my text. I had just reached this very page when I thought I heard the unmistakable sound of a chime whistle. Was this tome finally getting to me? No, there it was again but now much clearer. Quickly packing away the pages I had printed out and downing the dregs of my coffee, I walked out onto the platform. There, standing at the far end of Platform 2, was No. 70000 **Britannia** and her support coach, having just arrived from the West. I spent the next 15 minutes watching the doyen of this famous class, 'running round' her coach. Then, with daylight beginning to fade, the 'Pacific' – nameless and restored to the unlined black livery as originally carried until officially named at Marylebone station on 30th January 1951 – headed off westwards to gain access to the West Somerset Railway and await her next exploits out on the main line. I have to admit I felt very much as I suspect I had when I first witnessed one of the same class of locomotive (albeit resplendent in fully lined green livery) sixty years earlier.*

* I know, this is bound to prove a 'hostage to fortune'; almost inevitably there will be the odd error that escapes the combined efforts of both publisher and scribe!

Norman had positioned himself at the western end of Platform 10 (which led into Platform 9) to witness No. 70022 *Tornado* arriving at Temple Meads with the 1.00pm Plymouth- Liverpool (Lime Street).

19th September 1951

As with No. 70020, various records and recorded sightings of No. 70022 appear to be at variance as to when this locomotive entered traffic. The engine was noted in the erecting shop at Crewe with the boiler fitted on 14th July 1951. It was seen outside the Paint Shop awaiting painting on 12th August, yet some records state it entered traffic and was allocated to Laira just 4 days later! I suppose it depends on what is meant by 'entered traffic' but bearing in mind it had first to be delivered to Swindon for acceptance, the fitting of ATC, and running-in trials, perhaps another report which has the locomotive arriving at Swindon then transferring to Laira some weeks later may be correct? Obviously some further research and clarification is still necessary!

Another classic view at Temple Meads, this time at the 'London' end of the station. No. 5008 *Raglan Castle* approaches Platform 5 with the 9.15pm Wolverhampton (Low Level) to Penzance, better known as 'The Cornishman', which also conveyed through coaches to Kingswear. Scheduled arrival time at Temple Meads was 12.25pm. *3rd October 1952*

There were limited opportunities to obtain this view unfettered by other traffic entering, leaving or shunting stock over this busy section. This 'shot' was a 'near miss' – see the exhaust smoke just curling into the frame to the left! The upper storey of the flat-roofed Bristol Temple Meads East signal box can be seen above the rear section of the train. As to the formation of this train, the first three coaches are Hawksworth stock, possibly BTK, TK and CK. Next there is a Dining car, which appears to be of older lineage but doubtless refurbished, followed by three further coaches which may also be of Hawksworth design. These seven formed that portion of the train bound for Penzance, whilst the remainder (four or five coaches) were destined for Kingswear.

TEMPLE MEADS – ARRIVAL & DEPARTURE

An Easter Monday relief to the Up 'Merchant Venturer' rolls in alongside Platform 10 behind an unrecorded 'Hall' Class 4-6-0. Platform 10 continued north eastwards as Platform 9, providing a combined length of 1,340 ft. As with some of the other platform lines at Temple Meads, a scissors crossover mid-distance along No's 9 and 10, linking with the adjacent through line, enabled two trains to be accommodated at the same time. *19th April 1954*

More of Bath Road motive power depot can be seen in the left background and also the inevitable group of 'locospotters' congregated around the water column towards the end of island platforms 4 and 5, where the movements on and off shed could be observed. Those with good eyesight (or a cheap pair of binoculars) might also pick out the numbers of some locomotives which showed no sign of moving off shed. Closer to hand, the right side of the platform from which Norman Lockett took this photograph was designated No. 11, intended originally for Portishead line trains. Certainly by no later than the 1950s, it was more often used to load/unload covered vans. The houses forming the backdrop on the skyline include Bellevue Terrace and Higham Street, located at the eastern end of the Windmill Hill area of the city.

Another favourite location – towards the north east end of Platform 7 and looking across to Platform 9. The regulator of Bath Road (82A)-based No. 4084 *Aberystwyth Castle* has just been opened to get the 11.45am departure underway for a scheduled 2 hour non-stop run to Paddington via the Badminton line. Almost hidden in the shadow of the overall roof, an 0-6-0PT pauses on the adjacent through line, doubtless engaged in station pilot duties. *Monday 5th October 1953*

The overall roof was completed in January 1878 as the culmination of the construction of the new 'Joint' station, which had been planned in the late 1860s by the GWR, the Midland Railway and the Bristol & Exeter Railway. The latter company was absorbed by the GWR at the start of 1876, after construction of the station had commenced in 1871.

PATCHWAY TO CHIPPING SODBURY

Prior to the 1950s, Norman Lockett paid only a single photographic foray to the GW main line on the north side of Bristol and that was to the lineside near Pilning. He had also made one or two visits to the area around Yate. However, from the 1950s – following an initial visit made close to Winterborne – occasionally he visited the line between Patchway and Chipping Sodbury. On the following pages we have included a selection of views in journey order travelling eastwards.

We start this section with this view taken from an overbridge west of Patchway station, which features another Bath Road locomotive, No. 1011 *County of Chester*, nearing the end of a climb the better part of seven miles at 1 in 100, broken only by a half-mile 'breather' at Pilning. Norman failed to record any details of the train but noted the time as 1.40pm. My guess is that in all probability this was a Cardiff to Portsmouth (or Brighton) service which, if calling at Temple Meads and requiring a reversal of direction, means No. 1011 would have been replaced there. *28th September 1953*

Notice the difference in the levels of the Up and Down lines. The latter is the original (single) line opened in 1863 by the Bristol & South Wales Union Railway, which linked Bristol to New Passage, on the eastern side of the River Severn. Absorbed by the GWR in 1873, the route was used as far west as Pilning for the line leading to the Severn Tunnel, when opened in 1886. However, to ease the heavy climb eastwards from the tunnel, the additional line (the new Up line) was graded at 1 in 100 all the way from Pilning Junction to Patchway, rather than follow the gradient profile of the existing (now the Down) line, which included sections as steep as 1 in 68 and 1 in 90. Hence, the significant differences in the respective levels of both lines over this 3¼ mile section of main line. It also resulted in different lengths of the Up (1,760 yds) and Down (1,246 yds) line tunnels at Patchway. By the way, the line to the right of the train was a refuge siding, accessed from the Up Main Line just before Patchway station was reached. At some distance behind the rear of the train can just be seen the Up Home signal for Patchway Tunnel Signal Box (with the Distant signals for the diverging routes at Patchway below), the roof of which is also just visible.

PATCHWAY STATION

The summit of the climb from the depths of the Severn Tunnel is reached here at the western end of Patchway station. Class '57XX' 0-6-0 'Pannier Tank' No. 3643, allocated to St. Philip's Marsh, does its best to darken the sky as it works a short freight, possibly a trip or local working from Pilning into Bristol. *5th October 1953*

Prominent at the western end of the platform ramp is the Down Starting signal controlled from Patchway Signal Box, together with the Distant signal – the latter motor-controlled from Patchway Tunnel Signal Box.

Another impressive exhaust as Canton-based 'Castle' Class No. 5077 *Fairey Battle* breasts the top of the long climb with the 1.0pm Cardiff-Brighton. To the left, a westbound freight is held awaiting 'line clear' in the Down Goods Loop, the footplate crew just visible over the arm of the Distant signal. No. 5077 had only recently returned from a Heavy Intermediate overhaul at Swindon and is coupled to a standard Collett 4,000 gallon tender. Norman noted the time as 1.52pm so the 'Castle' was on schedule for its next booked call at Stapleton Road. *5th October 1953*

The 1.10pm Cardiff-Brighton (with through carriages for Portsmouth) was one of a number of trains on this route which omitted Bristol Temple Meads and the need to reverse direction there by running via the chord between Dr Day's Bridge and North Somerset junctions (see pages 62-63). Passengers for Temple Meads were required to change trains at Stapleton Road. No. 5077 would work through to Salisbury, returning home to Cardiff later the same day.

With just the tail of the train yet to pass over the summit of the eastbound climb from the Severn Tunnel, No. 7025 *Sudeley Castle* accelerates the 11.10am Milford Haven-Paddington through Patchway station. Booked for a non-stop run between Newport and Paddington, the time was noted by Norman as 3.50pm, so this train too was running to schedule. *5th October 1953*

The position more usually selected by Norman for his photographs at Patchway can be seen at the far end of the Down platform. This appears to have been the only occasion when he decided to include the station in a photograph. What looks to be a light engine is held in the Down Goods Loop awaiting clearance of the main line before heading towards Pilning. No. 7025 had been in service for just four years when seen here and only recently returned from a Heavy Intermediate overhaul at Swindon. From new, this locomotive remained allocated to Old Oak Common until August 1960.

Just 39 minutes after departure time from Newport (for a scheduled non-stop run to Paddington), an immaculate 'Britannia Pacific', No. 70029 *Shooting Star*, heads through the cutting to the east of Stoke Gifford with the Up 'Red Dragon' – the 7.30am from Carmarthen. Note that the fireman has turned on the water spray to damp down the coal in the tender. *19th April 1954*
'The Red Dragon' was run as a titled train between Paddington and Carmarthen from 5th June 1950. The coaches here are all in BR carmine & cream livery. All are BR Mk1 stock, except the Restaurant pair seen half way down the train (which are ex-GWR and can be identified by their roof destination boards) and the leading coach – a 70ft 'concertina' Brake Third of 1906-7. The thin carmine stripe just below the roof line did not suit coaches with toplights very well – it had to be broken for each of those small windows. Presumably something had happened to the usual BR Brake Third and this elderly example had been substituted. By the way, notice the pw man walking his 'length' and correctly facing any oncoming traffic – which is just as well as both 'boards' are 'off' (see the signal arms in the distance) for a Down train!

STOKE GIFFORD CUTTING

Immediately to the east of the former Patchway station, a junction facing Up traffic provides one route towards Stoke Gifford West Junction (the Patchway Loop Line), whilst the other route (classified as the Main Line) diverges towards Filton Junction. The latter, in turn, is linked to Stoke Gifford West to complete a triangular layout.

We are following the route towards Chipping Sodbury so, after traversing the 'Loop' from Patchway station and merging with the line from Bristol at Stoke Gifford West

Junction, we reach – just a little further to the east – what nowadays is Bristol Parkway station. Here, until 1971, were to be found the goods loops and numerous sidings which formed Stoke Gifford Yard, extending to just short of the far side of the overbridge seen in the background of Norman's photograph, above. Other than two short sections of level track, eastbound trains heading towards Swindon are faced with around 10 miles of climbing at 1 in 300 all the way to the summit near Badminton.

Fifteen minutes out of Temple Meads, No. 6019 *King Henry V* powers up the long gradient towards Winterbourne with the **11.45am Bristol-Paddington, a non-stop run scheduled, that year, to arrive in the capital at 1.55pm.** *29th May 1950*

My reason for the inclusion of so much of the background to the right side of this photograph will become evident on reading the notes accompanying the caption on the page opposite.

WINTERBOURNE

'The Pembroke Coast Express' (7.45am Pembroke Dock-Paddington) was another express scheduled to run non-stop between Newport and Paddington. Somehow, I doubt that a 'Modified Hall' was the customary class of motive power for this service and was here acting as a stand-in. However, No. 6994 *Baggrave Hall* has the train running to time as Norman photographed it, crossing Mill Road where the railway enters a cutting leading east towards Winterbourne station. *3rd August 1953*

As far as can be ascertained, Norman never made a print of this photograph. The reason, I suspect, was the inclusion of a thick unsightly cable stay extending diagonally into the side of the cutting on the extreme left. I have 'digitally' removed it!

Norman described the location featured on these two pages as being 'near Winterbourne' and, because this is a stretch of railway rarely travelled by this writer during the steam era, a degree of investigation was necessary to determine the exact whereabouts. Nowadays, much of the background is very different to that as seen here in 1950. The M4 motorway passes almost at right angles under the main line and carves a course across what then was the open countryside seen in the right background. Much of the fields beyond – rising gently to the skyline – are now covered by light industrial and residential development, the latter being part of the Great Stoke and Bradley Stoke area which form the north-eastern boundary of the Bristol conurbation. Seen protruding above the skyline near the right border of the first photograph, opposite, is a tall chimney serving – perhaps – a brickworks? The cutting seen in the distance is the eastern end of that featured in the photograph on page 35. Incidentally – and true to form – having identified the scene, I subsequently opened a copy of The Railway Magazine *dating from the 1950s and there was a photograph taken at the very same location!*

BELOW: 'The Red Dragon' storms past Winterbourne Signal Box. The exhaust from the BR 'Britannia' Class 4-6-2 obscures the small goods yard on the Up side of the line, with only the short siding serving a cattle dock visible. The express conveyed a Refreshment car eastwards from Cardiff, where the BR 'Pacific' had taken over the train. Unfortunately, Norman did not record the details of the locomotive from his position standing on the overbridge (Hicks Common Road) immediately to the west of Winterbourne station. It proved to be another of Norman's 'one-off' visits, possibly because, more usually, he shunned the opportunity for these high-angle shots. Still, it does show that the cleaners at Canton had done their customary very good job including a polish right across the top of the boiler. Although Norman failed to record the details of the locomotive, we can identify it as No. 70026 *Polar Star* – thank goodness for the invention of the 'perspective correction tool', which permits a scan to be manipulated sometimes sufficiently to reveal such details! As will be evident from these pages, soon after some of the new 'Britannia Pacifics' were allocated to the Western Region they became the first choice of motive power for both the Up and Down services of this express east of Cardiff. *28th September 1953*

RIGHT: Note that whilst the Up train was scheduled non-stop from Newport, the corresponding service in the Down direction called additionally at both Swindon and Badminton. Likewise, west of Cardiff, more calls were made by the Down train.

Table 5

TABLE 5

THE RED DRAGON
Refreshment Car Service (¶)
LONDON (Paddington), NEWPORT, CARDIFF, SWANSEA and CARMARTHEN

WEEK DAYS

London (Paddington)	..	..	dep.	p.m. 5A55	Carmarthen	.. .. ..	.. dep.	a.m. 7A30
Swindon	.. .. ..	..	"	7 25	Ferryside	.. .. ..	"	7A42
Badminton	.. ..	..	"	7 56	Kidwelly	.. .. ..	"	7A50
Newport	.. .. ..	..	arr.	8 47	Pembrey and Burry Port	..	"	8A 0
Cardiff (General)	.. ..	..	"	9 10	Llanelly	.. ..	"	8A10
Bridgend	.. ..	..	"	9 48	Loughor	.. .. ..	"	8A17
Port Talbot (General)	..	..	"	10 10	Gowerton North	.. ..	"	8A22
Neath (General)	.. ..	..	"	10 20	Cockett	.. .. ..	"	8A30
Swansea (High Street)	..	..	"	10 36	Swansea (High Street)	..	"	8A45
Gowerton North	.. ..	..	"	10 57	Cardiff (General)	.. ..	"	10A 0
Llanelly	.. ..	..	"	11 6	Newport	.. .. ..	"	10B20
Pembrey and Burry Port	..	..	"	11 15	London (Paddington)	.. ..	arr.	p.m. 1 0
Kidwelly	.. ..	..	"	11 27				
Ferryside	.. ..	..	"	11 35				
Carmarthen	.. ..	..	"	11 46				

A—Seats can be reserved in advance on payment of a fee of 1s. 0d. per seat (see page 31).

B—Except on Saturdays seats can be reserved in advance on payment of a fee of 1s. 0d. per seat (see page 31).

¶—Refreshment Car available between London (Paddington) and Cardiff (General), in each direction.

50

A lovely sunny mid-morning finds Landore-based No. 5958 *Knolton Hall* in charge of the 8.10am Swansea-York, on the long 1 in 300 climb approaching Lillyput Bridge, a mile or so east of Wapley Common and to the west of Chipping Sodbury. It was only since 1946 that this train had been rescheduled to run 'the 'long way round' via Newport, Swindon, Oxford, Banbury and Woodford Halse, passing along the Great Central main line to Sheffield, then via Pontefract to York. This journey was scheduled to occupy just 2 minutes in excess of 9 hours to complete! *3rd August 1953*

The formation of the train looks similar to the weekend version of the 8.20am, which used North Eastern Region and Western Region stock alternately. This is the WR train; it appears to have three strengthening Thirds on the front of the regular formation. All the coaches seen here ran through from Swansea to York. The locomotive was changed at Banbury, where it was serviced and awaited the corresponding Down service before returning to Swansea. This train ran via this route on every weekday from 1946 until 1954, then Mondays, Fridays and Saturdays only during 1955-56 and finally Fridays/ Saturdays only from 1957.

CHESTER

On Sunday, 22nd June 1952, Norman stopped off at Chester, a change of trains *en route* to a holiday in North Wales. Whilst at Chester, he took only two photographs, both featuring the same locomotive. There is some confusion as to which trains Norman photographed – possibly a case of some glass plates being returned to the wrong envelopes on which details are recorded. However, we are reasonably confident this photograph depicts the 2.55pm (Sundays) Birkenhead-Paddington setting off from Chester. 'Star' Class No. 4053 *Princess Alexandra* will have just taken over the train, which reversed direction following arrival from Birkenhead.

Norman also photographed No. 4053 arriving at Chester the same day, so this must have been a Sunday 'out and return' working for this Wolverhampton, Stafford Road locomotive, which had been built in 1914. It had just over another two years in service, remaining based at 84A, when records show it was sent to Swindon, arriving on 9th July 1954, withdrawal following just three days later. It was cut up at Swindon during the 4 week period ending 11th September 1954.

HATTON

ABOVE: Another 'one off' visit, mid-week on a sunny autumn day in 1952, found Norman at the lineside around Hatton, on the WR London-Birmingham main line. No. 7010 *Avondale Castle* (the third of the class to be completed at Swindon following Nationalisation) approaches Hatton station with the 9.20am (SX) Bournemouth West to Birkenhead (Woodside), a scheduled journey occupying just over 8½ hours – proof, if it was needed, that it was quicker (on paper at least) via the 'Somerset & Dorset' line if wishing to travel from Bournemouth to Liverpool! *15th October 1952*

RIGHT: An impressive sight as No. 6016 *King Edward V* sweeps down Hatton Bank with the 8.55am Birkenhead-Bournemouth; these Merseyside to South Coast services ran via Chester, Shrewsbury, Birmingham (Snow Hill), Oxford, Reading West, Winchester and Southampton. *15th October 1952*
Another of Norman's photographs from this same visit to the lineside near Hatton appears on the half title page.

YEOVIL

ABOVE: I mentioned in the Introduction to this book that the geographical spread would be more diverse than had proved possible in the first volume and, following visits to Cheshire and Warwickshire, here we are back in the south of Norman Lockett's 'home' county, at Yeovil. Looking over the northern parapet of the Sherborne Road bridge finds No. 4927 *Farnborough Hall* restarting the 9.26am Bristol, Temple Meads to Weymouth train from Pen Mill station. This service would next call at Maiden Newton (the junction for the branch line to Bridport), then Dorchester West, before reaching Weymouth with a scheduled arrival time of **12.09pm.** *7th October 1954*

Notice that only the Down Main Starting signal has been cleared; the Distant signal controlled by Yeovil South Junction remains at caution. The other Starting signal (left hand bracket as viewed here) authorises access to the short link line (the branch) to Yeovil Town. All of these three signals have sighting boards so that the arms can be picked out more easily against the background of the road bridge. To the left is a signal which controls movements from the south end of the platform serving the Up main line. This has a 'route indicator' capable of displaying any one of four different routes: to the Engine Shed, Up Branch, Down Branch and Down Main. At the time of preparing this caption (autumn 2011), Pen Mill still sports some semaphore signals controlled from the box just visible to the rear of the train, although nowadays the signals are of Southern Region upper quadrant design.

LEFT: We have to move forward, briefly, into the early 1960s to find a photograph taken by Norman at the lineside of the short but scenic ½ mile single line linking Yeovil Pen Mill and Town stations. Ex-L&SWR Drummond Class 'M7' 0-4-4 No. 30129, with a 'pull & push' set, is in charge of the 12.29pm (Sundays) from Pen Mill. The single journey time allowed for shuttling between the two stations was no less than 2 nor more than 3 minutes. *5th August 1962*

The author remembers being chastised by the late Dick Riley many years ago for using 'push & pull' – it was always 'pull & push' on the Southern!

'Large Prairie' No. 5157 pulls away from Yeovil Town with the 2.32pm branch line 'all stations and halts' service from Pen Mill to Taunton, an overall journey of some 16 miles, occupying an hour and ten minutes in which to enjoy the Somerset countryside, much of it across the Levels. The next halt would be at Hendford, a mile and a half farther westwards. The parcels coach (extreme left) is branded to work between Swindon and Weymouth. *7th October 1954*

For many years, Yeovil could boast three stations and a halt; Pen Mill (seen opposite), Yeovil Junction (on the SR main line), Hendford Halt (on the western outskirts of the town) and, seen above, Yeovil Town, which was a former joint SR/GWR station conveniently close to the town centre. The Town was (as is still the case at Pen Mill) an example of a station where one of the running lines was served on both sides by a platform face. Beyond the station footbridge in the distance, the line linking with Pen Mill passed to the right of the trees seen in the right background, whilst the line to the Junction turned sharply to the right. Notice, waiting in the nearside island platform, the Drummond class 'M7' 0-4-4T, a former L&SWR design long associated with the 'pull and push' trains which plied between the Town and Junction stations many times each day. To the extreme right of this view can just be seen a part of the Southern Region motive power depot. With so much 'going for it', this location must surely still exist in model form in some enthusiast's roof space or spare room? Hopefully so, for there is nothing left of the real thing, the station having been flattened and the site used for a car park!

BATH TO THE LIMPLEY STOKE VALLEY

'Castle' Class No. 5087 *Tintern Abbey* arrives at Bath Spa with 'The Merchant Venturer', which was booked as a non-stop run of 107 miles from Paddington in a scheduled time of 1 hr 46 mins. No. 5087, built (technically a rebuild) in 1940, was allocated to Old Oak Common where, other than visits to Swindon Works, it remained based until January 1962. It was withdrawn on 1st August 1963 when allocated to Llanelly. *27th September 1954*

Whilst, from the early 1950s, Norman took many photographs from the London end of the Up platform at Bath Spa, each featuring the arrival of a Down train, David has been able to discover only three taken from the same end of the Down platform! This is the best of the trio and although previously published many years ago, this is the first time the full width of the photograph has been reproduced. Notice the stub sidings each accessed via the small turntable. The heavy set of buffers was essential as, immediately beyond, there was a precipitous drop into the River Avon which passes under the railway at both this and the west end of the station. The Up platform, seen to the left, also included a bay at this end of the station. I recall it was used as the starting point for an afternoon local service to Chippenham at some time during the 1950s.

On a sunny Wednesday afternoon, No. 1010 *County of Caernarvon* passes through Sydney Gardens with the 1.18pm Paddington to Weston-super-Mare. This wonderful vista is here enhanced by the external appearance of No. 1010 (then allocated to Laira); this was the result of a visit to Swindon Works for a General Repair, the locomotive recorded as out-shopped only 5 days earlier. This would have been one of a number of 'running-in' turns before the 4-6-0 was returned to her home shed at Plymouth. *6th July 1955*

Norman managed to 'press the button' at exactly the right moment to capture the driver returning the waves of the young children assembled at the side of the line, whilst a pair of workmen pause from their labours to look over the top of the high retaining wall from the rear garden of a house in Sydney Road. By the way, don't be deceived by the roof boards into thinking that this train was an 'express'. The 1.18pm from Paddington was not scheduled to reach Bath until 4.03pm! An explanation follows on a later page. During 1839/40, Brunel produced various sketches of bridges and the like depicting his detailed proposals for this classic entry of the railway into Bath – the passage through Sydney Gardens. The completion of Box Tunnel enabled services to commence throughout between Paddington and Bristol from 30th June 1841. It is, perhaps, a sad reflection on today's society that this section of line has in recent years become one of the 'hot spots' for trespass. Consequently, in 2010, Network Rail announced the proposed erection of a safety fence along the public side of the low wall bounding the Up side of the line. NR announced that 'consultation' would include the opportunity for the public to state a preferred style of fencing, the choice being ornate Georgian, Victorian, or contemporary. As at autumn 2011, work on the fence has yet to commence. With electrification of this line now approved, some sort of fence will become inevitable and the 'open' views from the lineside gardens created by Brunel will be denied to future generations.

As the early evening shadows begin to lengthen, No. 5911 *Preston Hall*, with a surplus of steam, heads east along the very picturesque valley of the River Avon between Claverton and Dundas. The train is the **4.35pm Cardiff-Portsmouth & Southsea**, another of these through services which avoided reversal at Bristol Temple Meads by running direct from Stapleton Road towards Bath via Dr Day's and North Somerset junctions. The scheduled departure time from Bath Spa was 6.08pm, so with Norman recording the time as 6.15pm, the train is heading on time for its next point of call at Bradford on Avon. *12th May 1954*

This beautiful valley, which today still remains mostly unspoilt between Bathampton and Bradford on Avon, provides one of those rare examples in the south west where – for several miles – road, rail, canal and river occupy a roughly parallel course. No. 5911 is approaching the famous Dundas Aqueduct which transfers the Kennet & Avon Canal from one side of the valley to the other, crossing over both railway and river. In this view, the river runs westwards at the far side of the field immediately beyond the railway.

This location is less than a mile farther to the east from that featured opposite. No. 6945 *Glasfryn Hall* **approaches Fisher's Crossing, north of Limpley Stoke, and heads homewards with the 4.25pm Bristol to Weymouth. The track seen to the extreme left of this view is the single line to Camerton, which had closed the previous year. The branch had seen just 41 years of use, most of that for freight only.** *21st May 1952*

Part of the superb aqueduct at Dundas (to which I refer in the caption on the page opposite) can just be seen in the background but mostly obscured by the linesman's hut much closer to hand. Designed by John Rennie (the aqueduct not the pw hut!) and built in 1804, the structure is regarded by many as his finest architectural achievement. An award winning restoration was undertaken during 2002-04 which included removal of 'unsympathetic' repairs made over many years, most notably by the GWR (and, doubtless its successor) using engineering brick rather than matching (and much more expensive) Bath Stone!

The Camerton Branch ran parallel with the main line for the first quarter-mile or so north from Limpley Stoke station to the point seen here, where it veered off to head westwards along the Midford and Cam valleys. For much of its length, it was – without doubt – one of the most picturesque branch lines one could hope to find. Built primarily to serve the collieries around Camerton and Dunkerton, up to 8 miles to the west, the branch had seen just 41 years of use, most of that for freight only. All was not yet quite dead on the Camerton Branch, however, because just a few weeks after Norman's visit (above), the line would be used to provide many of the locations to feature in a film, a comedy to be entitled **The Titfield Thunderbolt.** *In fact, the location here was used for one scene. When David first emailed me a scan of this plate, I looked at the date and wondered whether his father had visited the area to scout for lineside locations where he might photograph some of the scenes being filmed by Ealing Studios. I hoped to see photographs by Norman of the locomotive which was to 'star' in the film, the historic Liverpool & Manchester Railway 0-4-0 named* **Lion,** *which had been resurrected from a museum and, for the duration of the filming, renamed* **Thunderbolt.** *Also, perhaps, the pair of '14XX' Class 0-4-2 tanks hired in from the WR by the film makers. No such luck. Perhaps, had he first met Ivo Peters by this date, things might have been different!*

A Return to Old Haunts

In April 1954, Norman paid a return visit to Plymouth which had been the base for his photography from 1934 to 1939. During that period, it appears he took only one photograph of the Royal Albert Bridge; and that without a train in sight! Now, although only a very brief return to his old haunts, Norman took some superb photographs featuring this famous structure which carries the single track railway high above the River Tamar and into Cornwall. Today, of course, all views of it as photographed here by Norman are overshadowed by the parallel road bridge opened to traffic in 1961.

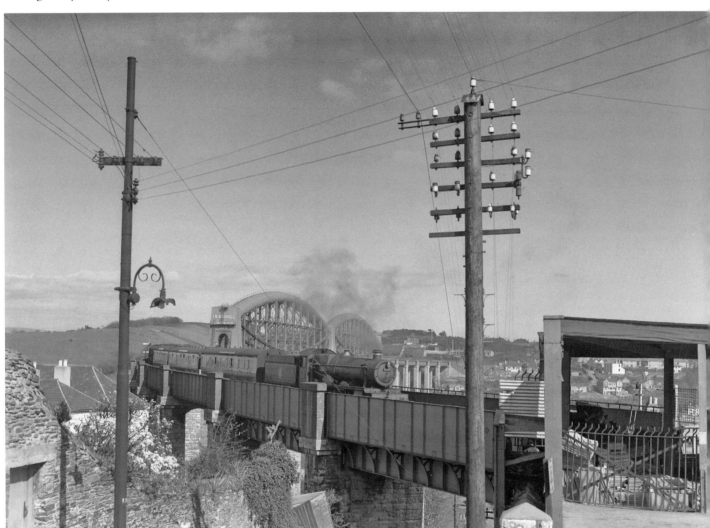

This, by any stretch of the imagination, is not the usual 'style' of Norman Lockett's photography – which makes it all the more fascinating. This view is from Albert Road, Saltash, which is crossed by the last of the spans carrying the railway around the sharply-curved approach into Saltash station from the two main spans. Laira-based 4-6-0 No. 5964 *Wolseley Hall* is about to regain double track. Norman recorded the train as being the 3.45pm Plymouth to Penzance. *15th April 1954*

Apparently this train was timed to provide a good connection off 'The Cornishman' for local stations west of Plymouth. An interesting variety of stock was included. The first three coaches carry roof boards which appear to have been reversed. Leading this trio of vehicles is a Brake Third of 1936, one of the earliest examples of a Collett large window 'sunshine' coach. Note how the smaller windows for the guard, luggage compartments and the external doors are all aligned with the tops of the larger windows. Next is another of Collett's large window designs, in this case a Composite dating from around 1938. In this design it is the lower edge of all the windows which are aligned. The third coach is an older Collett 'high waist' type. See how much smaller the windows are compared with the other two designs. The fourth vehicle may be a Siphon – it is difficult to be sure given the acute angle. Then (judging by the roof ventilators!) there are at least two more vehicles behind plus a van bringing up the rear. The latter might be a fish van, as one such vehicle – ex-Grimsby – was, I understand, sometimes conveyed on the final leg of its journey by this service.

The more you stare into this photograph the more detail comes to light. Look, for example, through that open-sided store to the right; you can see the post on which is mounted the lamp used during the hours of darkness to illuminate the lineside setting down post for the single line token. The net attached to the setting down post is also visible. Then there is the ornate-pattern street lamp, the shadow of which is cast onto the boundary wall of the property which is just out of picture to the left (nowadays 'The Two Bridges' public house but formerly 'The Royal Albert Bridge Inn', in the era before the road bridge was constructed across the Tamar) Finally, notice all those open fields which form the backdrop 'upstream' from the bridge. Just visible on the skyline (to the left of the wooded area) is the top of the tower of the parish church at St. Budeaux. Much of the hillside has long since been covered by housing development, including the Ernesettle area of the ever-expanding City of Plymouth.

BR 'Britannia' Class No. 70024 *Vulcan* reaches the end of the single line section on the Devonshire side of the bridge. The train is the 8.45am (Sundays) Penzance-Plymouth. *16th April 1954*
Royal Albert Bridge Signal Box controlled access to/from the single line section at the eastern end of the bridge, the block section from the box at Saltash being 924 yards in length. Not visible but passing under the second of the approach spans on this side of the bridge, was the Southern Region main line from Plymouth, which gained the eastern side of the Tamar to head northwards towards to Tavistock en route to Exeter. This and the following plate have been published before, many years ago, but – as with other such examples in this book – this is the first time the full width of the image has been reproduced. In 2011, Network Rail obtained listed building consent for plans to undertake, during the following three years, the most complex programme ever, estimated in the region of £10 million, to strengthen and fully refurbish the Grade 1 listed Royal Albert Bridge. Repairs will be made to corroded parts of the structure and efforts made to replicate the original design by using, for example, special bolts similar in appearance to the Victorian rivets.

A superb study of Brunel's Royal Albert Bridge bathed in sunshine on a cloudless spring day. No. 5978 *Bodinnick Hall* (with a tender still displaying evidence of pre-nationalised ownership) steams across the bridge with the Up 'Cornish Riviera'. Norman recorded the time as 'Noon', so the train was running to time for a scheduled arrival of 12.12pm at North Road, where No. 5978 would be replaced. *16th April 1954*
When making a print from the glass plate negative, Norman masked the left side in order to exclude the rather prominent telegraph pole. We decided to scan the full width of the image so as to include more of the spans which form the curved approach on the far side of the bridge. In so doing we can incorporate such long-lost features as the Saltash ferry, seen preparing to depart the slipway on the Cornish side of the river. Norman may have been fortunate to obtain an unobstructed view from this exact position; it looks as though somebody has only recently cut down some of the 'greenery' in the foreground!

SOUTH DEVON INCLINES

Various locations on the main line between Newton Abbot and Plymouth featured heavily in *Great Western Steam 1935-1949*, not least the inclines at Dainton and Hemerdon.

However, post-war, Norman made only two visits to these well known inclines which feature on this page and opposite.

This view from summer 1951 – but otherwise undated – shows Laira-based No. 7804 *Baydon Manor* attached ahead of an unrecorded 'Castle', on the lower part of the climb from Aller Junction towards Stonycombe and the summit at Dainton, with a Plymouth-bound train. The train is most likely a weekend excursion, as the roof boards on the coaches have been reversed to obscure what appeared when the stock was in normal use during the week. The milepost on the Up side of the line identifies the exact location, about three-quarters of a mile into the climb from west of Aller Junction.

At the start of 1948, Laira still retained six of the famous 'Bulldog' 4-4-0s, so long a feature on the South Devon Banks. By 1950, all of these had been either withdrawn from Laira or reallocated elsewhere (soon, in turn, to be taken out of service). No. 7804, transferred from St. Philip's Marsh to Laira during the 3 week period ending 15th May 1948, was amongst a number of this class which were moved to 83D to replace the 4-4-0s. Two more were allocated to Newton Abbot (83A) and all found use on 'piloting' amongst their duties.

The stock on this train is a modeller's delight when it comes to variety; the leading coach a 57ft 'toplight' Brake Third, an early example with wood panelling and flat bar truss underframe. Coach 2 is a Collett large window Third; coach 3 is a Collett 'high waist' 8-compartment Third, possibly a bow-ended design. Coach 4 is another Collett large window design, probably a Composite; coach 5 is a Dining car which has been modernised and is now running on 6-wheeled bogies. Coach 6 is another Collett large window design but too much obscured by the telegraph pole for it to be identified further. Coach 7 appears to be another 'toplight' (probably a steel panelled example as it appears to be sitting on a steel angle truss). The final coach (another partially obscured by a lineside telegraph pole) is possibly a Collett large window Brake Third.

Just as a reminder, the lineside milepost indicates the distance as measured by the original 'Great Way Round' (via Swindon, Bath and Bristol). The mileage from Paddington via the later direct route (but excluding the subsequent Westbury and Frome avoiding lines) was 20 miles 19 chains (say 20¼ miles) less.

No. 6001 *King Edward VII* blasts 'his' way up the lower part of Hemerdon Incline, most of which was graded at 1 in 42, with a relief 'Cornish Riviera Express', the running of which may have been necessary as this was Maundy Thursday. Norman noted the time as 12.32pm, so this 'relief' must have been running immediately ahead of the main 'Riviera'. The leading coach is a Collett 'high waist' Brake Third (possibly bow-ended); the second a Hawksworth design. Coaches three and four are Collett large-window types followed by a 'Dreadnought' (possibly the Restaurant car). The rest are too indistinct to identify. *19th April 1954*

This was a favourite location visited time and time again by Norman between 1934, when he moved to Plymouth, and 1939, after which he was transferred by his employer to manage various branches of Boots the Chemist during the Second World War. Post-war, this appears to be his only photograph here, taken during the visit to Plymouth immediately prior to the Easter weekend in 1954.

SHALDON BRIDGE -1

Those of you who have looked at our previous volume may recall we included a couple of Norman's photographs taken on the sea wall to the east of Teignmouth, when he first visited the town in August 1949. Four years later, Norman returned to this area with his camera, on this occasion venturing also to the west side of Teignmouth on a very blustery autumn day (see opposite page lower). Undeterred by the conditions, this proved to be just a 'taster' for what was to come, because Norman returned to this delightful seaside town on many occasions during the remainder of the 1950s invariably – it would appear – enjoying excellent weather. As a consequence, we have so many photographs it has made the selection of those to be included in this book all but impossible. Even so, although we must limit those to be included within these pages, we hope you will understand why this famous section of the former GWR features so prominently! The pictures on these two pages all show the line from or looking toward Shaldon Bridge, which carries the A379 coast road to Torquay across the Teign estuary.

A feature of this photograph and opposite (lower) is that Norman did not record full details; to be more precise – other than the date – David has been unable to find any information regarding this train, heading westwards under Shaldon Bridge! However, enlargement of the scan made from Norman's negative reveals the 'Modified Hall' as No. 6962 *Soughton Hall* (allocated to 81A). The 4-6-0 is carrying a 'Class B' headlamp code and the stock is LMR, so this may well be a through service or excursion from the Midlands. *5th September 1954*
Norman took this picture from a small grass-covered sandstone rock jutting out into the estuary, which can only be reached by passing under the arch (seen here) at the north end of Shaldon Bridge, from a location known as 'Polly Steps', just to the west of the docks at Teignmouth. The house seen partially obscured by the locomotive's exhaust above the Up side of the railway is the former Toll House, dating from the opening of the bridge in 1827. When built, originally in timber and to a length of 1,671 feet, Shaldon Bridge was said to be the longest in England.

RIGHT: Looking westwards or up-river, Newton Abbot's No. 5024 *Carew Castle* heads the Up 'Torbay Express' along the side of the estuary in the approach to Teignmouth. The small grass-covered rock from which Norman took the photograph opposite is clearly visible. Notice the solitary gas street lamp which borders Bishopsteignton Road, high above the railway. *7th October 1953*

BELOW: Looking in the opposite direction and nearly 3 hours after taking the previous picture, the weak autumnal sun had disappeared. The tide is still out as, with the impressive exhaust snatched away by a strengthening wind, No. 4089 *Donnington Castle* accelerates the 11am Paddington-Plymouth away from its call at Teignmouth. Norman recorded the time as 3.15pm, so the train was just a few minutes down on schedule which, doubtless, could be recovered on the fairly relaxed timings allowed for this service. *7th October 1953*

'*This was a badly scratched glass plate which we have done our best to repair digitally*'.

THE SEA WALL – 1

This has to be one of the most photographed railway locations in the British Isles, yet Norman took just this single shot here, much preferring to take up a position farther along the sea wall towards or beyond Sprey Point. So, although this photograph has been published before, we felt it merited inclusion here. Laira-based No.6816 *Frankton Grange* emerges from the East Cliff cutting and onto the sea wall with the 9.20am Kingswear to Exeter, passing under the lattice girder bridge which dates from 1883-4. The two signal arms are the Teignmouth Down Inner Home and, complete with a sighting board, the Down Distant for Teignmouth Old Quay (the latter signal box, being less than 500 yds beyond the box at Teignmouth station, also provided with an Inner Distant for the Down line). *13th April 1954*

Photography of Up line traffic here was (still is!) best undertaken during the earlier part of the day, before the track is put into the shadow cast by the cliff face. Nowadays, most of the tower of St. Michael's Church, seen in the left background beyond the East Cliff public shelter, is no longer visible when standing here; it is now masked by the construction of an additional storey over the former public shelter to accommodate the Teign Corinthian Yacht Club. Note the two lads standing near the entrance to the sea wall, just beneath the signal, notebooks in hand, whiling away part of their Easter holidays with a morning's 'loco spotting'. Nearly sixty years later, this location still attracts boys, young and old; indeed, the regular summer Sunday steam hauled excursions which traverse this line often attract substantial numbers of bystanders along this most famous stretch of line.

The masonry piers of the high lattice overbridge – Eastcliff Bridge – were built by the contractor Stevens of Ashburton, with the ironwork fabricated by the GWR at Swindon. This section, from this end of the sea wall to the station, was originally a tunnel accommodating the broad gauge single track opened as far west as Teignmouth at the end of May 1846. It was opened out when the line was doubled, by which date Brunel's infamous 'Atmospheric' Railway had been consigned to history. If, like this writer, you are fascinated by this coastal section of the WR main line to the west and wish to learn much more, I can do no better than refer you to an excellent book entitled **Exeter-Newton Abbot: A Railway History** *by Peter Kay (Platform 5 Publishing Ltd, 1993). Although I thought I had a reasonable knowledge of the railway history of the Teignmouth area, it proved only a minute fraction of the information contained in Mr Kay's very detailed book.*

Looking absolutely immaculate in the bright sunlight of a spring-time morning, Shrewsbury-based 'Castle' Class No. 5091 *Cleeve Abbey* **pulls away from a call at Teignmouth and heads, right time, towards Sprey Point with the 8.0am Plymouth-Liverpool (Lime Street) express. This service included coaches, put off at Crewe, for Manchester and, seen at the rear, a portion (departing 8.05am) from Kingswear, which had been attached at Newton Abbot. The leading coach, destined for Glasgow, also came off at Crewe, where it was transferred to the 1.30pm from Euston. No. 5091 had only recently returned from a Heavy General overhaul at Swindon. This had been one of only five of the 'Castle' Class temporarily converted to oil-firing between 1946 and '48.** *13th April 1954*

This photograph was a 'cert' for inclusion in this book, not only because of the condition of the locomotive but also because, despite having photographed trains since 1934 (with only the war years putting a temporary halt to his hobby), it was – as far as we have been able to ascertain – the first print which W.N. Lockett (William Norman) submitted for publication. It appeared in the August 1955 issue of 'Trains Illustrated'. David believes his father may have been encouraged to start submitting prints to publishers as a consequence of having joined the Railway Photographic Society. This was an organisation co-founded by Maurice Earley in 1922, which remained active for more than fifty years and attracted many accomplished photographers into its ranks. The main objective of the society was to raise the standard of railway photography. This was pursued by means of a portfolio which was circulated and into which members submitted their chosen print(s). Each member provided any comment (usually constructive criticism) on a standard form issued by the society, which found its way back to the photographer in question during the next circulation of the folio. The content was continuously refreshed by each member removing his print(s) and substituting one or more new examples each time the folio reached him.

ABOVE: After a brief visit to South Devon we return to north west Somerset and the area around Uphill Junction. This proved to be another 'one-off', a view from the Bridgwater Road overbridge looking north towards Uphill Junction. 'Castle' No. 5073 *Blenheim* heads under the flying arch forming Devil's Bridge with the 9.15am Liverpool-Plymouth, which included through carriages from Manchester and put off a portion at Newton Abbot for Torbay stations and Kingswear. *1st October 1953 Norman recorded this train as the 9.05 Liverpool (Central)-Plymouth. Unfortunately, I do not have access to the time table for winter 1953/4 but those for the preceding and subsequent winter services show only a 9.15am service from Liverpool (Lime Street). Devil's Bridge has nothing to do with Satan! It is named after a local landowner, some of whose property was purchased hereabouts by the Bristol & Exeter Railway to construct the new line which opened as far west as Bridgwater in 1841. The bridge has a span of 110ft and the height from rail to road level is 63ft.*

UPHILL JUNCTION

LEFT: Norman recorded No. 1011 *County of Chester* – allocated to Bristol, Bath Road (82A) – as being in charge of the 9.42am (Sundays) Chippenham to Exeter. On other days, this service ran only as far as Weston-super-Mare, arriving at 11.32am. However, on Sundays the service continued westwards after a wait of 7 minutes at Weston. It was due to pass Uphill Junction at 11.42am so No. 1011 was running some 8 minutes late when recorded here by Norman at 11.50am. Why this train commenced at Chippenham was an operating quirk for which I have been unable to establish any reason. *22nd May 1955*

A nice study of sunshine and shadow. The fact that, by mid-afternoon, the shadows cast by the trees extend onto the Up line probably account for this being the last of Norman's photographs taken from this position during this visit. No. 6869 *Resolven Grange* has come via the main line from Worle Junction – avoiding Weston – and heads towards Highbridge and home (the locomotive was based at Laira) with a Class 'H' freight. The leading open wagons contain what appear to be some large diameter drainage or conduit pipes, a reminder of those times when the railways still carried a very wide diversity of freight and minerals traffic. *29th September 1955*

Stanier Class '5' No. 45269 sets off, 7 minutes late, from Platform 14 at Temple Meads with the 8.20am (Saturdays) to Bournemouth West, which this Saltley-based locomotive worked only as far as Bath, Green Park. Later in the day, No. 45269 would doubtless take over a train northbound from Bournemouth via the S&D line. The other train which can just be seen waiting in Platform 12 and headed by another 'Black Five', No. 44843, is the 8.30am Bristol-Newcastle, also recorded as departing 7 mins late. *23rd July 1955*

I have included this photograph (linked with that opposite) because it serves as a reminder that Bristol, Temple Meads was a 'Joint' station. Following the major rebuilding works in the 1930s, more and more of the LM&SR services, terminating at or commencing from Temple Meads, made use of the platforms then numbered 12 to 15. Consequently, this part of the station became widely known as the 'Midland station' or 'Midland side'. The distant church spire is that of St. Mary Redcliffe. The signal box seen in the right background was Bristol Temple Meads Goods Yard box, which controlled one semaphore shunting signal, a couple of ground discs and the electric token on the single line section of the Bristol Harbour Goods Line that passed, unnoticed by many, behind the north side of Temple Meads station. Notice also, just visible at a lower level, a small part of the massive covered goods shed which had been built by the GWR.

SECTION 2
1955–1959

The observant reader may have noticed the content of this book has now reached 1955 – the year when the railway 'Modernisation Plan' was introduced by BR. We will never know whether, at that time, Norman Lockett decided photographing diesel motive power was 'not for him'. It is a fact, however, that he appears to have ignored totally their existence – at least during the period covered in this section of the book. Thereafter, there might be just a *very* occasional 'sighting'; usually no more than an incidental detail in the background of a photograph of a steam locomotive!).

In 1957, Norman was transferred to manage the Boots the Chemist shop in Milsom Street, Bath. He and his family (well those yet to 'fly the nest') took up residence in the city in September 1957.

David noticed, only recently, that there is a gap of about six weeks in his father's records of visits to the lineside during the summer of 1957. It would have been very unusual for Norman not to be taking photographs during that period of the year. David thinks his father's attention had been diverted to packing and other essential tasks prior to moving house. One consequence of the transfer to Bath was the opportunity for frequent evening photographic visits to Bath Spa station. As mentioned in our Foreword, it was during a visit to that station (in May 1956) that Norman had met, quite by chance, another railway photographer who lived in the city – Ivo Peters. The two men were to become lasting friends, often visiting the lineside together in pursuit of their hobby, invariably travelling in Ivo's (now famous!) Bentley.

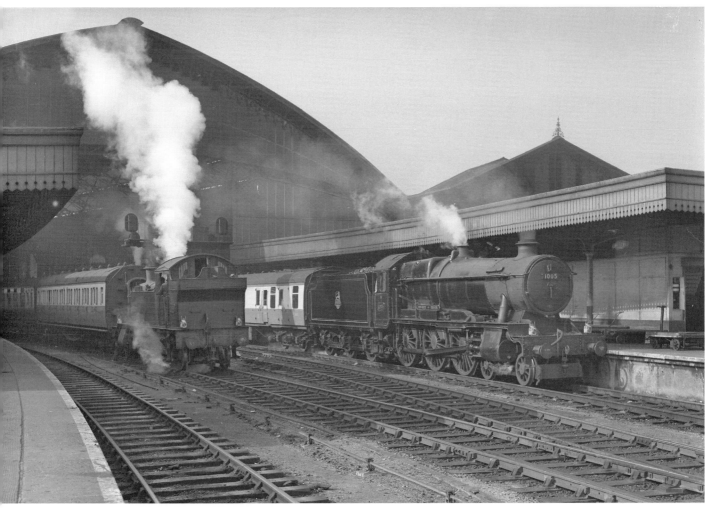

No. 1005 *County of Devon* **calls at Platform 9 with a Parson Street to Paddington excursion. A 'small Prairie' is seen passing through one of the centre roads, which were created when the original island platform under the classic overall roof was taken out as part of the rebuilding and enlargement of the station between 1930-35. Note the train shed to the 'Midland side' (see facing page) visible in the right background.** *1st October 1955*
Parson Street station is on the outskirts of Bedminster. I wondered whether this excursion, running on a Saturday morning at the start of October, might be a football special. However, on the day in question, it appears Bristol City were playing at home to Middlesbrough and the Rovers away at Lincoln – so that put an end to that theory! No. 1005, based locally at Bath Road, had been through the Works at Swindon the previous winter (into Swindon 6/12/54, out 12/1/55). It looks as though the cleaners at '82A' had put in some effort to spruce up the paintwork of the locomotive and tender, still resplendent in BR lined black livery.

This panoramic view shows 'The Bristolian', just a couple of minutes or so out from Temple Meads, at the start of a scheduled 1¾ hours non-stop dash to Paddington. This titled train service had been accelerated earlier in the year and No. 6015 *King Richard* III (which Norman recorded as the locomotive featured here) was one of the 'Kings' which had already been through the Works at Swindon and fitted with modified drafting arrangements – an improvement which led to the introduction of the faster post-war timing on this train. *3rd August 1954*

This is a bit of a 'cheat' by me, insofar that I have dropped back to 1954 in order to include this photograph! Norman had taken up position on the Barrow Road overbridge looking down at Dr Day's Bridge Junction. The lines curving away towards the left form the loop to North Somerset Junction, originally built so that traffic between London and South Wales did not have to reverse at Temple Mead. This, of course, was no longer relevant after such traffic could run direct via the Badminton Line. In more recent times, the loop was used by some South Wales-South Coast through trains to avoid reversal at Temple Meads and, certainly on some summer Saturdays, by a few of the North to West trains as a means of by-passing Temple Meads via the St. Philip's Marsh Avoiding Line. In the background, the original Bristol-Bath GWR main line completes the triangular layout here. Nowadays, this scene is dominated by an elevated section of the St. Philips Causeway (the A4320) which crosses the railway supported on concrete columns just beyond where Dr Day's Bridge Junction Signal Box had been sited to control this busy junction. The usual formation of 'The Bristolian' was seven coaches, which seems to be the case here, although the fourth coach appears to be a 70ft Centre Kitchen Restaurant car, whereas it should have been a Buffet car.

St. Anne's Park

'Castle' Class No. 5057 *Earl Waldegrave* emerges into the sunlight from what was originally known as Bristol No. 2 Tunnel (but later often referred to as St. Anne's Tunnel) with the 1.00pm Salisbury-Bristol, Temple Meads. Norman took this photograph from the 'country end' of the Down platform at St. Anne's Park station, which had been opened by the GWR on 23rd May 1898. *5th June 1957* When released new into traffic in June 1936, No. 5057 had been named Penrice Castle. *The following year, the GWR decided to transfer to the 'Castle' Class the names allocated in 1936 to the '32XX' (later '90XX') Class 4-4-0s, No. 5057 receiving the name which had been allocated to (but not carried by) No. 3214. The name Penrice Castle was reused on new 'Castle' No. 5081 in May 1939 but that locomotive, in turn, was renamed in January 1941. In a case of 'third time lucky', the name was used on No. 7023 in June 1949.*

FOX'S WOOD

The water troughs at Fox's Wood between Bristol and Keynsham is another location where we have been spoilt for choice, with Norman's many photographs taken here from the footbridge spanning the railway. ABOVE, Collett 0-6-0 No. 2251, in charge of a local freight, shuffles past the large water tank which fed the troughs whilst, BELOW, the fireman of No. 5034 *Corfe Castle* is a little late in lifting the scoop, having decided to top up the tender despite departing Temple Meads less than 10 minutes earlier with the 1.50pm Bristol-Paddington. *Both 1st October 1955*
In our GWR book, I commented that the troughs seen here were installed in 1895. That – I regret – was incorrect; they were brought into use at the end of June 1899 to replace an earlier set located a little farther west (reaching into the eastern end of Bristol No.2 Tunnel). Those seen here remained in use until May 1961.

NEAR BOX

A 'Castle' Class 4-6-0 (unidentified by Norman but we think it is No. 7036 *Taunton Castle***) speeds downhill towards Bath with the 4.15pm Paddington-Plymouth.** *25th May 1955*

I selected this photograph because I don't recall having previously seen another featuring this view looking in the Up direction from the footbridge near Shockerwick, a little to the south-west of Box. (Certainly it was a 'one-off' visit by Norman.) The road on the left is not a country lane but the A4, the London-Bristol trunk road which, in the pre-motorway era, was generally a very busy route. Whilst private car ownership was yet to burgeon, goods traffic was already carried in some quantity on the trunk and other major roads. Hence my amazement at the complete absence of any traffic in this photograph, even allowing for the fact that this was a mid-week early-evening scene. It's not how I remember it!

About a mile to the south, Farleigh Down Sidings provided a rail outlet to what became, in the late 1930s, a huge underground munitions storage site. A tunnel over a mile in length was necessary to link the sidings with the storage areas formed within a very considerable network of old stone quarries.

Looking in need of a clean, No. 7011 *Banbury Castle* **climbs the 1 in 120 gradient having just passed through Middle Hill Tunnel with the 7.50am Taunton-Paddington. This was a service which called at all stations between Bridgwater and Weston-super-Mare, then ran semi-fast to Paddington (including a 19 minute wait at Temple Meads!) calling at major stations only. Since released new in June 1948, No. 7011 had remained (until October 1959) a Bath Road allocation.** *18th June 1958*

Middle Hill Tunnel (198 yards long) stands to the west of the better known Box Tunnel. Both portals are of considerable height in a classical design, heavily decorated with segmental arches and sweeping flank walls. The cross-section of the tunnel reduces (just inside both ends) to a height and width more generally associated with that provided for the original broad gauge double track. The tunnel was constructed by Bristlington contractor George Findlater. Box Mill Lane Halt, which was opened in 1930, was located between the two tunnels, in a position much more convenient to serve the major part of the village than the original Box station, which was sited at some distance beyond the western end of Mill Hill Tunnel.

SWINDON WORKS & SHED VISIT

The Midland Area Group of the SLS had planned this special to run from Birmingham on Sunday 19th July 1955. The motive power requested was 'Star' class No. 4056 *Princes Margaret*, one of only three remaining in service. The outward run from Snow Hill station was scheduled to travel via Stratford-on-Avon, Gloucester, the avoiding line (Dr Day's Bridge Junction-North Somerset Junction) at Bristol, and Bath. The route proposed for the return run was via Didcot, Oxford and Stratford. The itinerary included visits to Didcot and Oxford mpds, in addition to the Works at Swindon – and all for the price of 21s 6d (£1.07½p)! Unfortunately, the tour had to be postponed, a consequence of the national rail strike. However, the event was rearranged to run on Sunday 11th September. Hauled throughout by 'Star' class No. 4061 *Glastonbury Abbey*, Norman photographed the Special preparing to pull out of the Works sidings at the commencement of the return run. The lighting conditions were far from ideal but this was too good an occasion to miss. The locomotive had been cleaned and the opportunity taken to reinstate the painted numerals 'GWR style' on the buffer plank, with the BR style cast numberplate removed temporarily from the smokebox door. At the time of the rearranged trip, No. 4056 was in the Works at Swindon undergoing repairs.

Note the two differing styles of the 2-wheeled motive power on the right; both riders apparently not the least bit interested in the visit of a 'Star', perhaps more intent on getting home at the end of a Sunday shift!

Whilst at Swindon, Norman also paid a brief visit to the motive power depot, where No. 6015 *King Richard III* was on display. We last saw this locomotive at Bristol, after having been fitted with improved drafting arrangements. Here, however, this 'King' had recently emerged from the Works as the first of the class to be fitted with a double blastpipe and chimney. Now a few days would be spent 'running in' on local services and, if all proved successful, the engine returned to 'his' home depot at Old Oak Common. Just a fortnight later, on Monday 26th September 1955, No. 6019 was given a run in charge of the 'Cornish Riviera' from Paddington to Plymouth when, with a load of 10 vehicles, a speed of 100 mph was recorded. Later that week, a top speed of around 108mph was claimed. By August 1958, all thirty members of the class had been similarly modified. *11th September 1955*

The locomotive seen in the background is 'Modified Hall' No. 6967 Willesley Hall resting between duties at its home depot.

TRAMWAY JUNCTION, GLOUCESTER

ABOVE: Gloucester-based No. 7006 *Lydford Castle* has both 'boards' clear for the passage out of Gloucester with the 11.45am Cheltenham (St. James)-Paddington. The driver looks back to check the rear of his train has cleared the level crossing. Almost hidden by the signal post (left), an 0-6-0 'Jinty' tank is engaged with some shunting work. *3rd October 1955*
The roof of Tramway Junction Signal Box is just visible over the tops of the second and third coaches. The much larger roof immediately beyond belonged to the former GWR motive power depot (seemingly only later officially referred to as 'Horton Road'). No. 7006 will have taken over this train, which included a Restaurant car, at Gloucester Central, where reversal of direction was necessary following arrival from Cheltenham. The short run from Cheltenham St. James station was usually handled by a tank engine and it was not unusual to see one of the '94XX' Class pannier tanks hauling up to twelve bogies along the four track section through Churchdown! Having just crossed, on the level, the former LM&SR route between Eastgate station and Engine Shed Junction (the latter adjacent to the former LM&SR mpd), No. 7006 is heading towards Gloucester South Junction. The train was booked to depart Gloucester at 12.07pm (Norman logged the time here as 12.10pm, so the train was 'right time') and, with calls at Stroud, Kemble, Swindon, Didcot and Reading, arrival at Paddington was scheduled for 3.0pm.

OPPOSITE PAGE TOP: No. 7003 *Elmley Castle*, a Landor-based (87E) locomotive, worked this train, the 9.15am Swansea-Birmingham, right through to its destination. The rest of the run was routed via the former GWR line through Cheltenham Spa (Malvern Road) to Stratford-upon-Avon and then Henley-in-Arden, the only three remaining scheduled stops before arrival at Snow Hill station. *3rd October 1955*
The leading coach is a 3 compartment 'toplight Brake Third'. It may well be an example sold to the War Office in WW1 and subsequently repurchased. It has a steel plated body but could originally have been wood panelled. The other four coaches are all BR Mk1s.

OPPOSITE PAGE BOTTOM: As a contrast to the other photographs included here (and by way of a 'thank you' to Richard Strange who has been so helpful in providing locomotive information for this book), Stanier Class '5MT' No. 44809 (17A Derby) sets off from Gloucester Eastgate with the northbound 'Pines Express' and is about to cross the former GWR lines at Tramway Junction. Progress is watched, briefly, by two railmen standing at the lineside. Bearing in mind the proximity of the mpd, doubtless they were from the 'opposite camp'! *3rd October 1955*
The Distant signal controlled by Engine Shed Junction Signal Box (sited at the junction with the northern end of the Gloucester Avoiding Loop) remains at 'caution' as No. 44809 heads for Cheltenham Spa (Lansdown), the next booked stop for this service. The Up 'Pines Express' (9.45am Bournemouth West to Manchester and Liverpool) was, I think, scheduled for a 12.58pm departure from Eastgate station. If so, according to the time as noted by Norman Lockett, the express was some 30 minutes late! Notice more shunting is in progress on the 'Midland' side in the distance.

WHITEBALL

The main line to the West Country passes between Somerset and Devon within the passage of Whiteball Tunnel (1,092 yards long). The west end of the tunnel marks the summit of the 9 mile climb which extends from east of Norton Fitzwarren. A little distance after exiting the west end of the tunnel, on a short length of level track, Whiteball Siding Signal Box was sited on the Down side, before the main line commences the long descent towards Exeter. Norman, who had last photographed hereabouts in 1948, revisited the area on a couple of occasions during the mid 1950s. It was opportune timing because, as related on the following page, the superstructure of the rather attractively designed original signal box here was destined to be replaced during late 1955.

With his hard work completed, the fireman of 'Castle' Class No. 5079 *Lysander* was able to take a 'breather'; the following 20 miles or so to the next booked stop at Exeter St. David's would call for no great effort. The train was the 10.50am (Sundays) Paddington-Paignton, a 'dated' service (running only during the height of the summer season). Norman noted the time as 2.30pm and with a scheduled arrival at St. David's at 2.36pm, *Lysander* must have been around 15 minutes down on the booked time passing Whiteball box. *28th August 1955*

No. 5079 was another of the class which, when built, had carried a name which was later changed. On release into traffic from Swindon in 1940, No. 5079 was named Lydford Castle. Just 18 months later, she was one of a group (No's 5071-82) to receive the names of aircraft associated with the 'Battle of Britain'. As Lysander, this engine had been one of the five 'Castles' modified to oil burning from early 1947 until autumn 1948. Modellers and students of GWR signalling might be interested in the close-up of the rear of the ringed-arm controlling exit from the Down refuge siding. This siding could be used to hold back trains of esparto grass or pulp destined for the paper mills at Silverton, until such times as the goods yard at Silverton was able to accept the traffic. However, to avoid delays on the main line when the train was later collected by a locomotive, a guards van had to remain on the rear for however long the wagons were stabled here at Whiteball. Notice also, in the distance, the white patch painted on the wall flanking the tunnel mouth; this was to enable the position of the arm of the Up Starting signal to be seen more easily from a distance against an otherwise indistinct background.

The Whiteball signalman obliges the photographer as the 1.30pm (Sundays) Paddington-Plymouth passes, a service with through coaches for Torquay and Paignton, and for Penzance. The first five coaches behind No. 6012 *King Edward VI* all appear to be BR Mk. 1 stock (BTK, TK, TK, CK and BTK) which formed the Penzance portion. Next should be an ex-GWR Dining Car and a BTK, both taken off at Plymouth. The last four coaches formed the portion to be put off at Newton Abbot for Kingswear. These too should be BR Mk. 1 design but are too distant to be certain. *28th August 1955*

This is another of Norman's photographs which has appeared many years ago. However, it is the only one which shows to advantage the original Whiteball Siding Signal Box provided by Saxby & Farmer and opened in 1876. This was severely damaged by fire during the evening of 28th November 1955, reputedly resulting from the over-zealous charging of a Tilley lamp! As will be seen, when Norman revisited this location the following spring, a replacement superstructure of a far more utilitarian design was in use. Notice how, originally, the telegraph pole route was taken 'over the top' from one end of Whiteball Tunnel to the other. In this view, a new pole route had been erected along the lineside (with the wires to be carried through the tunnel). It appears that wiring of the new route was about to commence.

Only the western end of the original signal box is in view as the occupant watches No. 6009 *King Charles II* pass by in charge of the 10.40am (Sundays) Paddington-Newquay and Falmouth. Note that the locomotive was missing the bonnet to the safety valves. Running in the wake of the 'Cornish Riviera', the 10.40am Paddington was scheduled to take only 5 minutes longer to Plymouth, despite the additional requirement to call at Exeter and Newton Abbot 'to take up passengers only'. *28th August 1955*

Notice the 174 milepost sited immediately opposite the signal box. Although the name of the signal box suggests a single siding, there were in fact two, a refuge siding on the Down side and the shorter facility on the opposite side; this latter was used, when necessary, for holding a banking engine until a path could be found to return to Wellington. More likely, only one of these sidings had been provided when the box was first opened.

ABOVE: Viewed from the overbridge just over a quarter-mile west of Whiteball box, No. 6029 *King Edward VIII* nears the summit of the eastbound climb on a hazy summer's day. This was the 10.20am (Sundays) Plymouth-Paddington, which also conveyed a portion – added at Newton Abbot – from Kingswear. The ascent on this side of the Blackdown Hills is less severe than encountered on the Somerset side but exists for a greater distance. Even so, No. 6029 still had a full head of steam. The relief line seen on the Down side extended from Whiteball to Burlescombe, the next block post to the west. *28th August 1955*

BURLESCOMBE

RIGHT: ... and now for something completely different! Norman took this picture, to include his youngest son Philip, at an underbridge on the private line which connected the large Westleigh Quarry with the goods yard at Burlescombe station, a distance of nearly a mile. I understand, by the time of this visit, the line had closed and the wagons, in very poor condition, were stabled awaiting scrapping. *28th August 1955*
A pristine example of one of these wagons appears in Private Owner Wagons A Tenth Collection *by Keith Turton, also published by Lightmoor Press in 2011.*

THE SEA WALL – 2

Class '28XX' 2-8-0 No. 3864, with a train consisting of mineral wagons, emerges onto the sea wall from Parson's Tunnel just after noon on a sunny spring day. No. 3864, allocated locally at Newton Abbot (83A) at the time, was one of the last of the class to be built at Swindon, in late 1942. These locomotives included some improvements made by Collett to the original design when construction recommenced with No. 2884, in 1938, after a break of nearly 20 years. As such, these later examples, numbered 2884 to 2899 and 3800 to 3866 were separately referred to as the '2884' Class. *9th April 1955*

This wonderful location (well, wonderful on a fine day!), which can be accessed from Smugglers Lane, Holcombe, or by walking the full length of the sea wall section from Teignmouth, became a favourite with Norman, who took so many photographs here. It is also full of memories for David Lockett, who recalls as follows:

'Ten years after my father took this photograph, I moved with my family to Teignmouth, to study at the Moorlands Bible College, Holcombe. The college was situated a little further back from the trees seen on the skyline above the western portal of Parson's Tunnel. It was quite an experience to feel the vibrations of the trains passing through the tunnel below us as we studied the Old Testament Prophets, New Testament Greek, The Gospels and The Letters of St. Paul. Later, after a career move just down the road to Torquay, I returned to Teignmouth in January 1971 to teach at The Beacon School, where I became the Headmaster in January 1975. It was soon after my retirement in 1987 that I met up with Mike and we set about publishing some of Norman's steam railway photographs. As we did so, it became very apparent that the Teignmouth area was such a favourite place for his photography in the '50s, the extent of which I had no idea, having left home in 1954.'

Staying with the freight traffic theme, this time we are looking westwards just beyond mid-distance between Eastcliff and Sprey Point. BR Class '5' 4-6-0 No.73032, built at Derby just two years earlier, was of a batch (No's 73030-9) originally allocated to the Scottish Region. Transferred to Bristol, St. Philip's Marsh (82B) during the period 4 w/e 3rd October 1953, the locomotive is here working towards Exeter with a long train of vans. *9th April 1955*

This was Easter Saturday; notice the elderly lady in her 'Easter bonnet' (!) gave not even the briefest glance towards the passing train. Not so the two girls, although perhaps it was the fireman – complete with beret – who was more the attraction than the BR 4-6-0? This appears to be one of very few photographs taken by Norman to feature a BR class other than the 'Britannias' working on WR metals.

When Norman made a print from this negative he masked both sides, that on the left for about a fifth of the full width of the glass plate. So here, for the first time, is the complete image which has the advantage of depicting, for the only instance as far as we have discovered amongst Norman's archive, the complete length of Teignmouth Pier, including the landing jetty at the seaward end. This superb study – one of this writer's favourites – features Laira-based Churchward 'Mogul' No. 5376, which dated from 1919, heading eastwards with an early morning freight along a deserted sea wall (just how Norman would have wished it!). *21st June 1955*

In order to reproduce this photograph to its original full width and so feature the complete pier in the background, it has been necessary to 'fill in' two vertical narrow strips of the negative where the glass plate was secured in position in Norman's camera by two clips. I hope the result is not too obvious but, having done this, I had better note for posterity those various parts of the pier which are here visible but have long since been removed! First to go was the middle pavilion (seen to the left of the signal post) in the latter part of the 1950s. The landing jetty was demolished in 1963, whilst the large ballroom (at the end of the main pier) was pulled down in 1975, although it had long ceased to be used as a venue for dances and had gradually deteriorated. However, the main pier is still extant and must be one of very few to which access can today be enjoyed without payment. Standing guardian over the scene, in the background, is the distinctive tree-covered rock headland known as The Ness. Now, back to WR steam …!

'THE SOUTH WALES PULLMAN'

We now move to South Wales and a couple of shots of the Pullman service introduced between Paddington, Newport, Cardiff, Port Talbot and Swansea from 13th June 1955. The view, ABOVE, shows the Down train (9.55am ex-Paddington) arriving at Newport behind 'Castle' Class No. 5084 *Reading Abbey* whilst, BELOW, eight days earlier, No. 5060 *Earl of Berkeley* was in charge setting off from Cardiff General. All seats had to be reserved in advance, with passengers paying a supplementary charge to use these services, for example 7 shillings (35p) for First Class between Paddington and Newport. *12th & 4th October 1955 The GWR had dallied with Pullmans at the end of the 1920s, some being included amongst other stock on Ocean Liner expresses between Plymouth Millbay Docks and Paddington. Then followed, briefly, the 'Torquay Pullman Limited', an all-Pullman service between Paddington and Paignton. The Western Region's 'South Wales Pullman' proved more successful and, from September 1961, the steam-hauled train was superseded by the diesel-electric multiple unit 'Blue Pullman' services.*

Another of the titled trains serving South Wales was 'The Red Dragon'. Here, the Up service (7.30am Carmarthen-Paddington) pulls away, right time, from Newport at 10.21am behind No. 5005 Manorbier Castle. 3rd October 1956

Even without the benefit of seeing the smokebox numberplate, hidden here by the train reporting numerals, No. 5005 could easily be recognised (by those 'in the know') by the small fitting protruding from the front of the casing above the inside steam chests. Apparently, this was a remnant from an earlier era during the 1930s when, for a short period, this locomotive was subjected to some streamlining which included the front of the smokebox. (An illustration of No. 5005 in 'streamlined condition' can be seen on page 27 of the first volume). The fitting, which can be seen clearly in Norman's photograph, had been provided to secure the frame into which train reporting numerals were slotted, as these could not be carried in the traditional position whilst the streamlined front to the smokebox remained in existence. Unlike Cardiff station, Norman obviously took a liking to the platforms at Newport, especially here at the north-east end where he returned on several occasions. Those buildings fronting Mill Street, which paralleled the railway, included the County Café, a congregational chapel, a 'chippy' and (seen to the right) the 'George & Dragon' (a Simonds' house). Most were swept away in the name of progress around the mid 1960s, for the provision of a Royal Mail Sorting Office, which, in turn, has since been closed. Notice, parked on the left of the nearside platform, the Morris 8 car and also a lorry belonging to Santon Water Heaters (a trade name which still exists in the 21st century).

'Castle' Class No. 5050 *Earl of St Germans* restarts the 9.10am Liverpool-Plymouth from Hereford (former Barrs Court) station. Norman recorded the time as 12.40pm, so with a 'booked' departure on weekdays at 12.39pm, the train was 'to time' and about to pass Ayleston Hill Signal Box. *20th June 1956*

Norman stopped off briefly at Hereford en route to a holiday in Shap. This might have been to change trains, as this was his only photograph taken here on this occasion. He failed to record the other two locomotives – a Collett '32XX' 0-6-0 and a Stanier 'Black 5' 4-6-0. Prominent in the left foreground is a twin tank gas reservoir wagon, probably an ex-LM&SR example. As well as gassing (splendid phrase) Restaurant cars with gas cooking facilities, they were also used for refilling the gas tanks of coaches retaining gas lighting. These included, for example, many auto trailers, which remained gas lit until they were withdrawn from service. The above photograph is dated just nine days after the introduction of the summer time table, so this might be an appropriate point to record that, as of that date, Third Class was abolished on BR and 'upgraded' (in name if nothing else) to Second Class – was it really that long ago!

TRAIN '208'

No, nothing to do with good old Radio Luxembourg but the reporting number used (Saturdays excluded) for the 9.10am departure from Liverpool (Lime Street)! This was booked to be formed of a portion for Plymouth, which included a dining section (the stock of which alternated between WR/LMR), and the remaining stock destined for Paignton. A corresponding

train (with the same reporting number) ran on Saturdays (9.15 ex-Liverpool, the Paignton coaches extended to Kingswear) and on Sundays (10.40am ex-Liverpool to Plymouth/Kingswear, with a portion from Manchester to Kingswear added at Crewe). Based on these two photographs of 'Train 208', the actual formation sometimes differed from that which was shown 'in the book'.

No. 5050 *Earl of St Germans* was obviously a favoured locomotive for this service during the summer of 1956, for here 'he' is again, this time approaching Platform 5 at Bristol Temple Meads. According to Norman's note of the time of day, the arrival here was about 8 minutes late. As was invariably the case with Salop-based top-link engines, No. 5050 was in immaculate external condition. This was a 'double-home' turn which, in 1956, was worked on alternate days between Shrewsbury and Newton Abbot by locomotives from those two depots. This being a Wednesday, No. 5050 would work back from Newton Abbot to Shrewsbury the next morning, probably with the 8.0am Plymouth-Manchester and Liverpool. *12th September 1956*

If I recall correctly, the end of this platform was another favoured location for the many 'locospotters' who congregated at this station in the post-war steam era, although only the more adventurous would proceed (as Norman has done here) beyond the top of the platform ramp. One of my lasting memories is that of the 'odour' (I will put it no more lucidly!) emitted – not from the large gasometer seen in the background – but from the chimney of a local pie factory, which pervaded this end of the station whenever there was a strong wind blowing from a certain direction. However, with my local station at Trowbridge having a substantial bacon & pie factory (Messrs Bowyers– sadly no more) located 'next door', I was used to enduring such 'delights'! Anyway, locospotters at Temple Meads never remained too long in any one location; they were constantly on the move in an attempt to see most of what was going on at this busy station. Speaking of 'locospotters', this phenomenon burgeoned amongst the male youth of the 1950s due, in no small measure, to the regular publication of the Ian Allan 'abc' of British Railways Locomotives, handy pocket-sized booklets – one for each BR Region (herewith the cover of the 1950 Western Region edition, RIGHT). Each contained details of all locomotive classes and listings of every locomotive for the appropriate Region. They became invaluable, not only to locospotters but to the likes of Norman Lockett who used them as a ready cross reference to check and record (where appropriate) the name of any locomotive he had photographed. It is interesting to note that the 1950 WR 'abc' was published too early to record the revised choice of names allocated to the last three members of the 'Castle' Class to be completed later that year – concluding appropriately with No. 7037 Swindon.

THE GOLDEN VALLEY, STROUD – 1

In 1956, Norman made what appears to have been the first of several visits to various lineside locations in the Golden Valley, to the east of Stroud. In this first photograph, having called at Stroud station, No. 5037 *Monmouth Castle* gets to grips with the easier lower section of Sapperton Bank, in charge of the 11.45am Cheltenham-Paddington. The immaculate condition of the locomotive was a credit to those responsible at its home depot, Worcester mpd (85A). As such, it might be difficult to envisage that No. 5037 would be paying a visit to Swindon Works for a Heavy Intermediate overhaul less than three months after Norman took this picture.
This and the two photographs opposite were all taken on 24th September 1956. Unfortunately, as will be seen, although the sun had broken through an autumnal mist when Norman took this first picture, later in the day – as witnessed opposite – the conditions became somewhat more overcast.

OPPOSITE PAGE TOP: The appearance of No. 7816 *Frilsham Manor*, a locomotive then allocated to St. Blazey (83E), on the 2.40pm Gloucester-Swindon, may well have come as a surprise to Norman. This, however, was explained by the locomotive having just paid a visit to Swindon Works (recorded as 7/8/56 to 18/9/56) for a Heavy Intermediate overhaul. This was obviously a service used as one of a number of 'running in' turns to test the engine 'on the road', before dispatch back to its base in Cornwall. You will notice only a partial repaint had been considered necessary on this visit to Swindon.

OPPOSITE PAGE BOTTOM: CLASS '57XX' 0-6-0PT No. 4628 spent most of its working life based at Gloucester (85B), before transferring to Worcester (85A) at the end of 1960. The train is obviously a 'Chalford Motor' (Gloucester to Chalford and return, stopping at all stations and halts along the route up the Stroud valleys) but Norman failed to record any details and, most unusually, not even the time he took this photograph. As far as David Lockett can ascertain, his father never made a print from the glass plate negative; possibly he considered the lighting conditions were too poor to warrant a print. All these years later, it makes for an interesting subject, especially as Norman did not expend too many glass plates on pannier tanks!

WESTON-SUPER-MARE GENERAL & LOCKING ROAD STATIONS

Despite his move to Bath, Norman still made visits back to his home town. However, it appears he strayed less frequently to those parts of the local lineside visited in earlier years. This and the following two pages are scenes taken from the Drove Road overbridge, where the lines serving the General and Locking Road stations merged. Norman took views looking westwards (towards both stations) and looking over the opposit parapet at traffic arriving in the Down direction. This has prove to be another location where we have been spoilt for choice as t which to include of Norman's many fine photographs taken here

A Whit Sunday excursion brought the 'City of Plymouth Holiday Express' to Weston-super-Mare. The weather looked set for a good half-day on the beach. Having set down the passengers at the General station, No. 7022 *Hereford Castle* drew forward in order to propel the stock into Locking Road, where the train would be berthed to await the return working later in the day. The finger raised by the driver suggests the train will be set back into 'No. 1' road – or is it some other sort of gesture he is making to the signalman! *25th May 1958*

This trip may have 'borrowed' the special headboard because, from memory, these 'Holiday Trains' were first run from several major cities in the mid to late-1950s. They picked up at several smaller towns close to their point of origin. More usually, they ran on five consecutive days in early August. Such excursions sometimes followed routes otherwise unavailable other than by changing trains – Trowbridge to Swanage via Salisbury, Wimborne, Broadstone and Hamworthy Junction (a 'Somerset & Wilts Holiday Express') remains etched in this writer's memory.

OPPOSITE PAGE BOTTOM: Collett 0-6-0 No. 2261, based at St. Philip's Marsh (82B), is signalled into Locking Road station with an excursion. Below the signal arm, a 'stencil indicator' displayed the number of the Locking Road platform into which the train would be routed. During at least a part of the 1950s, some of the return empty coaching stock of the many excursions from Bristol to Weston-super-Mare were worked back to Temple Meads, via the St. Philip's Marsh Avoiding Line. This enabled Temple Meads to be entered from the London direction and, having collected another load of passengers, for the train to set off again facing towards the seaside resort. *18th May 1959*

Of the several photographs Norman took from this vantage point, I decided to include this example because it included the sign seen to the left of the lineside. It read 'Drivers must reduce all engine noises to a minimum in this area and must not allow steam to blow up'. This was in deference to the staff and pupils at nearby Locking Road School (the site of which has since been redeveloped). The smoke in the distance appears to originate from a lineside bonfire.

On Whitsun Bank Holiday, No. 4978 *Westwood Hall* approaches its destination with the Down working of 'The Merchant Venturer'. This was the 11.15am departure from Paddington, which called only at Bath Spa and Bristol, Temple Meads, before a scheduled arrival at Weston General at 1.56pm (10 mins later on Saturdays). No. 4978 (a Taunton allocation) will have brought the train forward from Temple Meads. *26th May 1958*

UPHILL

The speed of No. 7000 *Viscount Portal* is eased down in order to turn away from the main line at Uphill Junction and take the Loop line into Weston-super-Mare. The train is the 8.0am Plymouth-Liverpool, which Norman timed here at 10.45am, so a 'right time' arrival would be made at Weston General station at 10.50am. Note the very high overbridge carried on a flying arch; this is the structure – Devil's Bridge – photographed (see page 58) from the opposite side on an earlier visit made by Norman. *5th August 1957*

I mentioned on page 83 how, on alternate days, a Salop-based locomotive worked south with the 9.10am Liverpool-Plymouth (which included a portion to Kingswear), returning the next day from Newton Abbot with the 8.0am Plymouth-Liverpool which included a through coach for Glasgow. Other than on Fridays (when a separate train was run), this northbound service included a Kingswear-Manchester portion. These 'double-home' workings were shared between Salop and Newton Abbot locomotives. One source shows No. 7000 was based at Newton Abbot from new (May 1946) until May 1959, although several others record a brief transfer to Canton (4 w/e 18/5/57 to 4 w/e 10/8/57). During that same short period, the engine was reported by one source to have visited Swindon Works (23/5/57 to 9/7/57). These two sets of dates are very similar and any transfer to Canton and/or visit to Works cannot be unconnected – but which is correct? All records agree that, in May 1959, No. 7000 was transferred from Newton Abbot to Gloucester.

OPPOSITE PAGE TOP: The first Monday in August 1957 was obviously another busy day at Weston judging from the activity seen here, although the lack of any shadow suggests it was not the best of peak-time holiday weather! No doubt No. 7217 (87E) had worked an excursion from the Swansea area and here pulls away from Platform 2 at Locking Road with empty stock. Another of these powerful 2-8-2Ts, No. 7250 (82B), heads a line-up of other motive power which has been turned and watered (or are waiting to do so) at the facilities provided on the Up side of the line. *5th August 1957*

The development of the stations at Weston is a little too complex to describe in any detail here. Suffice to say that the main (later General) station opened with the Loop Line in 1884 and replaced the second of two earlier termini served by a branch leading from the main line via an entirely different route. From July 1897, the GWR used an excursion platform built near the goods yard. The further growth of this traffic later saw this facility treated as a separate station, named Locking Road, from 8th April 1914. However, it only became wholly independent from the main station when it was rebuilt to the form seen here in the mid 1920s, specifically to handle an increasing volume of excursion traffic to the town. Being the closest West Country resort to the Midlands, Weston has always proved a popular destination for holidaymakers as well as a favourite for large numbers of 'day-trippers' from Bristol and the surrounding areas. This remained the case until, by the start of the 1960s, scenes such as that seen here quickly disappeared, as a combination of car ownership and cheap foreign holiday packages saw off most of the traffic which had been the preserve of the railways. Locking Road station closed on 6th September 1964. It hardly goes without saying that the site is now occupied by a Tesco supermarket and a large car and coach park!

OPPOSITE PAGE BOTTOM: Moving about 1¾ miles south of Weston General station, this view is a 'one-off' by Norman, looking in a northerly direction from the overbridge at Uphill Junction. 'Modified Hall' No. 6997 *Bryn-Ivor Hall* regains the main line from the Weston Loop with a Bristol-Taunton local service. The signalman can just be seen inside the box, whilst his car is parked in the shade of the trees to the rear.

This is another of a small number of plates which lack details of date and time as normally recorded by Norman but can be dated by cross reference to other of his negatives to late summer/early autumn 1957.

THE RETURN OF *CITY OF TRURO*

In January 1957, the famous 4-4-0 *City of Truro* was removed from York Railway Museum and taken to Swindon Works, where it was overhauled to full working order and its original running number 3440 restored. Following some successful 'running in' turns in late-March, the locomotive was used on various enthusiasts' specials, the first between Wolverhampton and Ruabon on a train organised by the Festiniog Railway Society. The 'North Somerset Rail Tour', organised by the Railway Correspondence & Travel Society and run on Sunday 28th April 1957, must have been amongst the earliest of the tours to make use of No. 3440. The special commenced at London, Waterloo and the 4-4-0 took over at Reading for the run to Bristol.

Having photographed the train earlier at Bath Spa, Norman was able to examine *City of Truro* at leisure whilst the locomotive was serviced at Bristol, Bath Road. Here it remained whilst the RCTS tour continued behind other motive power before returning to Temple Meads. Norman photographed No. 3440 from several angles but, in each case, the proximity of the water column and 'fire devil' prevented an uncluttered view (*and I didn't think it at all appropriate to digitally remove these features!*). The style of the livery which Swindon had bestowed on the 4-4-0 and its tender attracted some diverse comments amongst a few purists during the following months. *28th April 1957*
The tour continued westwards from Temple Meads behind a pair of Ivatt 2-6-2T's (and a separate rake of coaches) to visit the Bristol Harbour line, Wrington and Highbridge, from whence the 'S&D' was penetrated for a short return run to Burnham-on-Sea. All of which – together with some operational matters – contrived to delay the start of the return from Highbridge to Bristol by some 57 minutes.

ABOVE: With *City of Truro* back in action, and attached ahead of 2-6-2T No. 5528, the return journey from Bristol commenced with a run over the section of line from which the title of the tour was derived, although (as reported in the *Railway Observer*) some wag had suggested it be called the 'Somerset Straggler'! Here, highlighted by the rays of a setting sun, the special is seen near Pensford on the run towards Radstock West and Frome. *28th April 1957*
Norman recorded the time as 6.55pm. How he got out to this rural area on a Sunday evening is unrecorded. He must have endured a long wait here because, as related above, departure of the train from Temple Meads was rather later than planned! After using the chord at Frome which by-passed the station, the special ran to Westbury where No. 5528 was removed. City of Truro then returned the train to London (Paddington) which, through no fault of the locomotive, was reached 74 minutes late. Perhaps, as subsequently noted in the RO, as events turned out, the suggested alternative title for the train might have proved more suitable!

RIGHT: A Sunday excursion saw *City of Truro* travelling much farther westwards, working throughout from Swindon to Kingswear and back. Here, on the outward run, the special enters Uphill Cutting immediately to the west of Uphill Junction. *19th May 1957*
No. 3440 worked the train unassisted. On the return journey, where a reported speed of 83mph was attained at Wellington, the locomotive suffered some mechanical problems late into the run, which caused the train to be brought to a premature halt at Chippenham. There, the passengers were transferred to a following public service.

CLASSIC TEMPLE MEADS – 1

A sunny Wednesday afternoon spent at Temple Meads, during what must have been the final week of the summer 1956 time table, provided conditions ideal for photography. In this picture, taken from Platform 10, the Up 'Cornishman', the 10.35am Penzance to Wolverhampton, is seen arriving into Platforms 7/8 behind No. 5003 *Lulworth Castle*. Norman recorded the time as 4.08pm, which was the booked *departure* time for the train, so obviously it looked set to depart about 5 -10 minutes behind schedule, depending on how efficiently the staff handled the station stop. *12th September 1956*
Note: The numbering of the platforms at Temple Meads quoted by me in these pages are those as existed from late February 1934, until renumbered following rationalisation of the station in the mid 1960s. Notice the lads sitting on the 4-wheeled parcels trolley towards the end of the platform – I bet that brings back memories for some of you!

Mid-day departure. No. 5043 *Earl of Mount Edgcumbe*, for many years allocated to Old Oak Common, restarts the 10.20am Taunton-Paddington from Platform 6. We see here two of the five new platforms provided in the 1930s and note that, in contrast to the original train shed visible in the right background, the additional platforms were the traditional open style, with covered awnings to provide some protection from the elements. *18th June 1958*

Withdrawn on 16th December 1963 and sold to Woodhams at Barry on 30th April 1964, No. 5043 was purchased by the Birmingham Railway Museum in 1973 and moved to Tyesley to provide a spare boiler for No. 7029 *Clun Castle*. However, in 1996, the trustees of the BRM announced a project to restore No. 5043 to main line running condition. This scheme came to fruition on 3rd October 2008, when the locomotive moved under its own steam for the first time in forty-four years. So both No. 7029 and No. 5043 have been saved. More recently, a highlight was the use of *Earl of Mount Edgcumbe* to celebrate 175 years of the Great Western Railway. On 17th April 2010, this 4-6-0 headed a special – 'The Bristolian' – non-stop in both directions between Paddington and Bristol Temple Meads, a re-enactment of this famous titled train from the era depicted within this book.

'82A'

uring the latter years of the 1950s and into the '60s, if Norman paid a visit to a motive power depot it was usually as a member of the Bath Railway Society or, as here, in the company of Ivo Peters. This was a visit made on Sunday 16th August 1959 when, doubtless, activities 'on shed' were somewhat less hectic than the previous day – a very busy summer Saturday.

mongst the last of the class to be uilt, in 1950, No. 7033 *Hartlebury astle*, Above, had been serviced and rned following arrival at Temple eads in charge of train 'No. 212'. he locomotive was then stabled in ont of the running shed, Right, in mpany with No. 6986 *Rydal Hall* and o. 1009 *Country of Carmarthen*, both at that time – Bath Road engines.
th August 1959

n summer Sundays during 1959, '212' is the train number allocated to the .30pm Paddington to Weston-super-are, which the Old Oak Common gine hauled as far as Bristol. No. 7033 is ex-works just two months earlier d, during that visit to Swindon, was ed with a double chimney and twin astpipe. I understand, at the time, the comotive was considered the 'pick the bunch' of the 'Castles' based at IA', so the Sundays 12.30pm from ddington, which was booked to arrive Temple Meads at 3.40pm, would have rdly taxed this 'flyer'!

CLASSIC TEMPLE MEADS – 2

Churchward 2-8-0 No. 4701 arrives at Temple Meads with a relief working of the Up 'Merchant Venturer', running about 12 minutes ahead of the main train. The engine was an Old Oak Common allocation, so may well have worked this train right through to Paddington. These 2-8-0s had become a regular sight on through passenger services on Saturdays during the height of the summer season; to see one on such duties on a weekday was a much less frequent occurrence. *3rd August 1959*

Norman recorded 2-8-0 No. 3803 as having worked this empty stock train from Weston-super-Mare. As the train is facing westwards on the through road between Platforms 2 and 4, it must have arrived via the St. Philip's Avoiding Line from Temple Meads West to North Somerset Junction. Earlier in the year (w/e 28/2/59), No. 3803 had transferred from Llanelly (87F) to Gloucester (85B). *3rd August 1959*

Norman may have discounted this photograph because of the unfortunate juxtaposition of the arm of the water column and the smokebox of the engine. However, I wished to include the picture as a tribute to all those dedicated enthusiasts who have ensured the working future of this 2-8-0 which, following purchase from Woodhams in November 1983, was taken to Buckfastleigh. There, after a lengthy overhaul, No. 3803 was returned to steam in 2005.

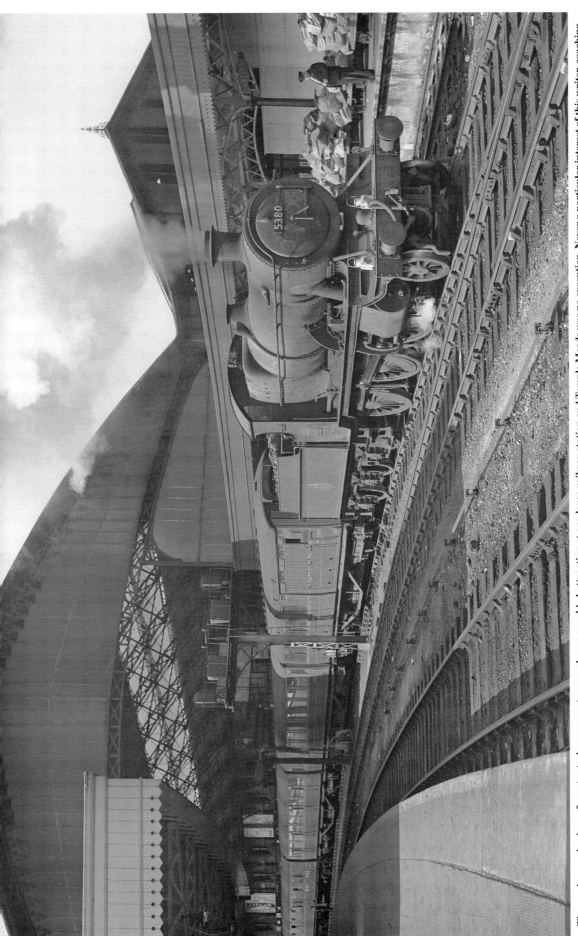

The comings and goings of empty stock movements were always an added attraction at any large railway station and Temple Meads was no exception. Never a particular interest of this writer, coaching stock of all former 'Big Four' companies could be seen at this regional crossroads. Churchward mixed-traffic 'Mogul' No. 5380 draws forward from the overall-roofed section on one of the through lines between Platforms 7 (left) and 9 with empty stock which included some Gresley ex-L&NER coaches. The leading coach looks to be a Brake First Corridor, with two compartments only and guard's duckets, built in 1930 to Diagram 142. Note the mailbags piled up on the platform trolleys; the large Royal Mail Sorting Office adjoined the station and – as a regional centre and railway crossroads – mail traffic was, for many decades, very much an everyday feature at Temple Meads. This later transferred to a purpose built facility at Bristol Parkway but mail traffic has largely today been lost from the railway and the site has now been converted by Network Rail for use as a training centre for engineering staff.

No. 5380, allocated to Didcot when photographed by Norman, dated from 1920. Modifications included the fitting of outside steam pipes as seen in this view. You will notice that, even in steam days, the sunshine sometimes penetrated the glazing in the fine overall roof of Wyatt's train shed, some of which can be seen to advantage here. Much glass had been replaced following the severe and many air raids suffered by Bristol during the Second World War. Another of this writer's abiding memories of Temple Meads station from the 1950s was the sight of the 'wheel tapper' and the sound emitted when, one by one, the rim of each wheel along the full length of a rake of coaches was struck using a long-handled hammer.

ABOVE: No. 4961 *Pyrland Hall* emerges from Twerton Tunnel, at 264 yards much the longer of the two tunnels situated on the outskirts of Bath, about 2 miles west of Bath Spa station. Norman didn't record details of the train but, with the time noted as 5.45pm and No. 4961 allocated to Reading, this was most likely the celebrated 2.35pm Paddington to Weston-super-Mare (via Devizes!), for which see page 107 for more details. *11th July 1956*

TWERTON
TUNNEL

RIGHT: Based at Bristol, St. Philip's Marsh, 'Mogul' No. 6360 emerges into the early evening sunshine with a Bristol-bound Class 'D' freight. *11th July 1956*
This, the most westerly of the two Twerton Tunnels, has portals built to a most attractive Gothic style, comprising a high arched opening surmounted with an embattled parapet and flanked by octagonal turrets. It is now a 'listed building'. Can you begin to imagine such thought being given to the design of a tunnel portal if built today!

This wider and more distant view looking towards the tunnel mouth features Laira-based 'Castle' Class No. 5089 *Westminster Abbey* **heading home with the 4.15pm Paddington-Plymouth, a service which conveyed a portion for Torquay and Paignton.** *22nd May 1956*

Flanked by Carr's Wood, see how well Brunel's design sits into the surrounding landscape. It looks particularly impressive when bathed in the early evening sunshine. Norman had taken up a position on the trackbed of what had been a refuge siding controlled from the nearby Twerton Tunnel Signal Box The latter closed on 20th November 1960. I had wondered if the lad seen standing at the side of the formation between the two nearest telegraph poles was Norman's youngest son, Philip. However, David says not, so it must be a local lad, perhaps from the group seen closer to the tunnel mouth.

There can be few finer backdrops visible from the platform end of a city station. No. 1014 *County of Glamorgan* (allocated to Bath Road) crosses the River Avon bridge at the eastern end of Bath Spa with the 2.33pm Portsmouth to Bristol. The train was on time but the schedule was hardly demanding and, after taking over at Salisbury, a pause was made at every station and halt (Avoncliff only excepted) until the destination was reached at Temple Meads. The locomotive was yet to be fitted with a double chimney and improved draughting. *30th May 1956*

Note the nearest house in the left foreground and the row of dwellings in the right background (as seen beyond the smokebox of No. 1014). These are all of brick construction which is rather unusual in a city famous for its stone architecture. By the way, when electrification of this line becomes a reality, I dread to think what effect overhead wires and all the associated infrastructure will have to this classic view.

'RUNNING-IN' TO BATH!

ABOVE: Here, on a different occasion, is the Down 'running-in' turn, the 5.0pm Swindon-Bristol, Temple Meads. No. 5066 (allocated to 81A) had arrived at Swindon Works named *Wardour Castle* but left renamed *Sir Felix Pole*. Pole, who had been the General Manager of the GWR between 1921 and 1929 had died in January 1957. This locomotive happened to be in the Works at the time the decision was made to honour his memory. *21st August 1957*

No. 5066 was recorded 'in' and 'out' of Swindon Works from 24/5/57 to 20/8/57 for a Heavy Intermediate repair. I suspect that I am not alone in thinking that the Hawksworth 4,000 gallon flat-sided tender coupled to the locomotive on completion of its recent overhaul detracted from the otherwise superb lines of the single chimney 'Castle' Class engine.

RIGHT: Another classic scene and an interesting study in sunshine and shadow. Truro-based No. 7823 *Hook Norton Manor* passes through Sydney Gardens on the approach to Bath Spa following a 'General Repair' at Swindon (recorded as 7/3/56 to 12/4/56) on the same service used to 'run in' engines before returning to their home shed. *18th April 1956*

It looks like a different smokebox (or at least the door) might have been fitted during the locomotive's overhaul. It is showing 84J (Croes Newydd), somewhat remote from 83F (Truro)! Another of the 'Manors', No. 7817, had been at Swindon 11/1/56 to 9/2/56 for a General Repair and that was allocated to 84J. Might the smokebox from that engine have been overhauled and fitted to No. 7823?

In the late afternoon, Severn Tunnel Junction (86E)-based 2-8-2T No. 7223 heads down the main line west of Bathampton with a lengthy Class 'H' freight. For very many years these impressive locomotives were a regular sight hereabouts, working heavy trains of coal between South Wales and Salisbury, and returning with empties or, as here, mixed freight traffic. No's 7202 and 7205 were regulars on this route. *20th September 1958*

Goods loops were provided here in 1942 on both sides of the running lines. This end of the loops and the associated signalling were, until 1957, controlled by Bathampton West Signal Box; the other end from the original box. The latter, adjoining the Down platform at the station, also controlled the junction with the line along the Avon Valley towards Bradford-on-Avon. Both boxes were replaced by a single new structure at the junction in September 1956 and the Up loop was shortened at the western end. The Down loop was taken out of use in September 1970. Notice the mark between the two signal arms on the left; not a flaw on the negative as I first thought but an aircraft!

BATHAMPTON

RIGHT: Having turned southwards from the main line, No. 4982 *Acton Hall* accelerates the 10.10am (Sundays) Cardiff to Portsmouth away from a permanent 15mph speed restriction across the junction and around the sharp curve leading into the Limpley Stoke Valley. This train called at Bristol Stapleton Road and avoided Temple Meads, enabling Canton-based No. 4982 to work through to Salisbury. It was a service which, when necessary because of Sunday morning work in the Severn Tunnel, departed Cardiff and Newport an hour earlier and travelled via Lydney and the Severn Bridge, necessitating the use of a lighter class of locomotive. No. 4982 had been a very recent reallocation from Ebbw Junction to Canton (recorded as during 4 week period ending 19/4/58). Most of the stock is in the maroon livery introduced from 1956. *13th April 1958*

The first ¼ mile post measured from the junction can be seen to the left of the points, which accessed a siding. Whilst No. 4982 could now be

accelerated from 15mph, note the permanent speed restriction indicator positioned to the right, reminding the driver of a maximum permitted speed of 40mph as far a milepost 1¼. Progress along the route of this very picturesque line was subject to several such permanent restrictions.

Looking in the opposite direction to that seen at the bottom of the previous page, 2-6-2T No. 4166 approaches the junction with the main line with a local service from the direction of Bradford-on-Avon. Norman didn't record any details but the engine is carrying a Westbury (82D) shedplate and was allocated there from December 1955 until the following summer (to Weymouth 3 w/e 16/7/55). Judging by the trees, this photograph was taken in the winter or early spring of what must have been late 1955/ early '56. On the right is Holmes Timber Yard, served by its single siding provided from 10th October 1922. The points to this siding (again seen in the previous photograph) were controlled from a ground frame released from the signal box.

Norman was standing adjacent to an occupation road crossing which provides access from Tyning Road to Bathampton Farm, on the east side of the line. Note the tower on the skyline; this is 'Brown's Tower', a folly built in 1848 by a local quarry owner, Mr Wade Brown. Visit this same location nowadays and only the very top section of the tower is visible above the crown of the trees. No. 4166 ('5101' Class) was new from Swindon in October 1948 and initially allocated to Tyesley (84E). It was the first of the class to be released in BR black livery, complete with red, cream & grey lining to the tank sides and bunker.

Class '43XX' 2-6-0 No. 6320 sweeps around the curves about a mile before reaching the junction at Bathampton, with a Bristol-bound train details of which Norman failed to record. However, the time was 4.30pm, the locomotive was allocated to Westbury (82D) and the 3.50pm Westbury to Bristol was due off Bathampton at 4.28pm, so that's a fair bet! The 'Mogul' displays evidence of a recent visit to Swindon (30/11/56 to 15/1/57 for a General Repair) whilst the provision of stock appears more than generous for a local stopping service. *22nd May 1957*

This is a photograph published before but to get the full benefit of this superb scene we have included the full width of the scan taken from the glass plate negative. The railway follows the river and the two are never far removed all along the valley, as is the course of the Kennet & Avon Canal (unseen here). The latter twice passes over the railway between this point and Avoncliff, a few miles farther south. Notice the permanent speed restriction indicator just to the rear of the train. This marked the start of the same restriction as mentioned on page 102 but from the opposite direction. The wooded margins of the Avon Valley provide a delightful backdrop whatever the time of year but nowadays this journey can, at certain times of the day, prove to be sheer purgatory to passengers packed like cattle into a two-coach Class '150' courtesy of First Great Western (it's not just you city commuters who suffer, you know!)

BRADFORD-ON-AVON

An unidentified 'Hall' Class 4-6-0 passes through Bradford-on-Avon with the 4.18pm (Saturdays only) Weymouth Town-Cardiff. This service also included portions to Cardiff and to Birmingham from the Quay station at Weymouth, which combined with the train at Weymouth Junction. The Birmingham coaches were detached at Westbury to run via Chippenham, Swindon and Oxford to Snow Hill.
18th July 1959

The ringed armed signals authorised exit from the Up refuge siding to (right) the Up main line and (left) into the goods yard at Bradford-on-Avon. Access to the yard was sited immediately beyond the bridge over the River Avon which, although not visible here, passes under the line at just about the position occupied by the rear coaches of this train. Also hidden (in the shade on the left) a foot crossing at which location this writer retains his earliest recollection of a steam locomotive. Although long since devoid of all freight facilities, the passenger station has retained most of its original features and is much used, not least because of some excellent staffing and an enthusiastic band of 'friends', who keep the station and its floral displays in excellent order. As this caption is prepared, a Government study has been released listing this station's staffed ticket office as one of 675 in England and Wales which is recommended should be closed and replaced with machines. What a way to encourage rail travel!

HOLT JUNCTION

No. 4962 *Ragley Hall* (81D – Reading) has just completed the section of its journey from Paddington to Weston-super-Mare which traverses a single line; note the fireman is checking he had placed the hoop with the single line token onto the 'bulls horn' (setting down post) rather than it falling to the ground. Yes, this was the infamous departure from Paddington (2.35pm in 1957), an express (according to the positions of the head lamps) which 'turned left' at Reading and travelled by way of Newbury, the single line from Patney & Chirton via Devizes to Holt Junction, then double track via Bradford-on Avon and the Limpley Stoke Valley. The main line was regained at Bathampton. Here, at Holt Junction, the 'express' was recorded passing 'right time' at 5.00pm, a mere 2hrs 25mins into a marathon which took nearly 4¼ hours to complete. *21st August 1957*

The passenger facilities at Holt Junction comprised an island platform on the line between Thingley Junction (west of Chippenham) and Bradford Junction (just north of Trowbridge on the line from Bathampton to Westbury). As mentioned above, it was also the junction for the line to Devizes which linked into the Westbury-Reading ('Berks & Hants') main line at Patney & Chirton. Both were frequently used as diversionary routes when, for whatever reason, either of the direct WR routes to the West were unavailable. This remains the case today with the (now singled) line from Thingley to Bradford Junction. The Devizes Branch, however, together with Holt Junction, was closed on 18th April 1966.

WESTBURY

Hauling a rake of BR Mk 1 stock in 'chocolate & cream' livery, 'Castle' Class No. 5092 *Tresco Abbey* arrives at Platform 2 at Westbury with the westbound 'The Royal Duchy'. The signal box – Westbury North – controlled the junction of the lines from Heywood Road Junction on the 'Berks & Hants' line and, seen bearing away to the left under the road bridge, the line to Hawkeridge Junction on the original route via Trowbridge. *21st August 1957*

It has been suggested that when BR relaxed the policy as regards the corporate livery of coaching stock and permitted the return to some regional liveries, it was on the basis this could apply only to 'titled' services. If true, that might explain why – in the following months – the WR introduced some newly titled trains! 'The Royal Duchy' was one such example when, early in 1957, the 1.30pm from London Paddington to Penzance and the 11am corresponding service in the opposite direction were given the title. Who remembers 'St Ivel Cheese' when it was 'Fresh up from Somerset'. The advertisement under the running-in board at Westbury was appropriate because, for very many years, some of the range of 'St Ivel' dairy products were produced and distributed from a factory just up the road from Westbury station (in Wiltshire!).

FROME

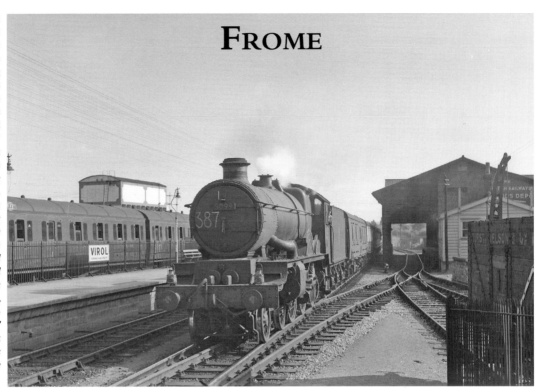

Running exactly to time, the 3.40pm 'Channel Island Boat Train' from Weymouth Quay to Paddington arrives at Frome behind No. 5099 *Compton Castle* of Old Oak Common. Calling previously only at Yeovil, Pen Mill, this train continued from Frome non-stop to Reading (to put down passengers only), before a scheduled arrival at Paddington at 7.32pm. *6th August 1957* *For an important limited stop express, a call at the town of Frome (rather than a romp eastwards via the 'Avoiding Line') might appear somewhat curious. However, the train carried mails from the Channel Isles (the connecting steamer service having departed Jersey at 8.15am and Guernsey at 10.30am) and that bound for Bristol and beyond was put out at Frome and transferred to the 5.55pm Frome-Bristol. This travelled via the North Somerset line, the train (comprising just two non-corridor coaches and carrying Class 'A' headlamps!) calling only at Radstock and Pensford. Arrival at Temple Meads was in time to transfer mail to the 'Northern Postal'.*

COGLOAD

Laira-based No. 6023 *King Edward II* speeds towards Cogload Junction with the Down 'Cornish Riviera Express'. *10th October 1953*
This locomotive was saved from the cutter's torch (just – the rear driving wheels having been 'torched') by the Barry Steam Locomotive Action Group in 1982, then sold on to Messrs Harvey's of Bristol before eventually finding its way into the ownership of the Great Western Society. Over the past twenty years, they have completed a total rebuild which included casting a new set of driving wheels. The restored locomotive moved under its own power for the first time on 20th January 2011 and entered traffic with an official launch ceremony at Didcot on 2nd April, in the blue livery which was used on this and other top link locomotives for just a few years in the late 1940s/early '50s. It is intended No. 6023 will return to the main line in 2012.

BREWHAM SUMMIT

These photographs are both rather a mystery because although listed by Norman there are very few details! We know it was a Saturday during 1958 and, from the dating of other photographs listed and having regard to the profusion of lineside flora and the height of the grass it's a fair bet the time of year is June/July. The location is Brewham summit situated between Witham and Bruton, so in terms of correct geographical sequence, they really should appear between the two pictures on the previous page.

LEFT: *'Brewham (S.O) W of England-Padd. Castle'* is all Norman left us for this one! Gross enlargement of the high resolution scan reveals the 4-6-0 to be Old Oak Common – based No. 5093 *Upton Castle*. Train No. 123 was more likely referring to an earlier Down working and has not been replaced with No. 387 for the return to Paddington. If so, possibly this is the 3.45pm ex-Weymouth, the 'Channel Island Boat Express'. This low angle shot certainly emphasises the change in gradient at the top of Brewham summit.

BELOW: 'Modified Hall' Class 4-6-0 No. 5978 *Bodinnick Hall* heads over the summit of the westbound climb at Brewham Signal Box. The train is the 4.35pm (Saturdays only) Bristol, Temple Meads-Weymouth which, if running to booked time, should be passing this location at around 5.50pm. No. 5978 was allocated to Weymouth (71G) but transferred to Swindon (82C) during the week ending 23/8/58.
The single siding on the Up side enabled an assisting locomotive to be refuged if, having banked a freight from either direction, a return path was not readily available for the light engine on this busy main line.

'FORTY STEPS'

No. 5099 *Compton Castle* is featured again, this time whilst accelerating the Down 'Royal Duchy' towards 'Forty Steps' after a call at Taunton. Norman recorded the time as 4.18pm and departure from Taunton was scheduled for 4.13pm, so the train is just two or three minutes behind time. *26th September 1957*

This and one other shot taken the same afternoon from the long footbridge (known locally as 'Forty Steps') straddling the railway here represent the total of Norman's efforts from this viewpoint. I suspect he would not have liked that heavy wire stretching across the eye line. Even so, not only was this the locale where a good friend of mine misspent some of his younger days 'loco spotting' but it also includes the factory (Avimo – the large building on the Up side of the line – where optical and other precision instruments were manufactured) where his future father-in-law worked!

THE WESTBOUND CLIMB TO WHITEBALL TUNNEL

A long term allocation of Shrewsbury (84G), 'Castle' Class No. 5073 *Blenheim* attacks the 1 in 80 gradient at Marlands on the final stretch leading to Wellington Tunnel with the 9.10am Liverpool-Plymouth. Note the Friesian cattle grazing in the lineside field, totally oblivious to the passing train. *2nd April 1956*

When preparing each book from the Norman Lockett Archive, David generally emails me scans without including any details. This avoids him having to replicate Norman's original notes for lots of photographs which do not get selected by me for inclusion in the book. The initial lack of any details enables me to test my knowledge as to the location featured and, for a time, this one had me beaten. The background looked familiar but if, as I thought, this was on Wellington Incline, surely the telegraph poles were on the wrong side of the line? Eventually, the 'penny dropped'; since Norman last visited the location in the late 1940s the telegraph route had been renewed and repositioned from the other side of the line! Hence all those newly creosoted poles and bright new insulators.

This represents another visit to the lineside (during the summer or early autumn 1957) following which any notes made by Norman appear to have been lost. No. 6025 *King Henry III* looks absolutely splendid in charge of the Down 'Cornish Riviera Express', here attacking the final 100 yards of the 1 in 80 climb to Wellington Tunnel. The gradient eases to 1 in 127 for the passage through the tunnel, at the far end of which the summit of this challenging climb is reached. Whereas in earlier visits Norman had always photographed from the Up side of the line, here he has transferred to the other side, south of the underbridge at Marley. Just visible on the skyline (near right edge) is the tower of Holy Cross Church, serving the village of Sampford Arundel

No. 6025 (the number and name again determined by enlarging the scan made from the glass plate negative) was allocated to Laira and had returned from Swindon Works in late March 1957 from a Heavy Intermediate repair, which included fitting a twin blastpipe and double chimney. Interestingly, from the 9th to 12th October 1957, the locomotive was recorded at Newton Abbot for a Light Casual repair. For such a short visit this would have been something fairly minor but, perhaps, beyond the capabilities of Laira to resolve.

WHITEBALL SIDINGS

No. 6021 *King Richard II* passes Whiteball Siding Signal Box with the Down 'Cornish Riviera Express', and commences the long descent towards Exeter. The train was due past this point in a minute under 2½hrs after departure from Paddington at 10.30am. Norman recorded the time as 1.05pm, so the 'King' was just a few minutes down on right time. *22nd April 1957*

I have included this scene because, unlike his previous visits, on this occasion Norman photographed the view looking towards the western end of Whiteball Tunnel from the overbridge adjacent to the signal box. His more usual approach was to climb down closer towards or at rail level. Notice, the replacement signal box superstructure and new telegraph pole route (both referred to on page 73) now in use with the old poles removed. Also the white patch on the left flank wall of the tunnel (provided to make the Up Starting signal more visible from a distance) is now far less prominent, having become partially obscured by accumulated soot and grime. The low retaining wall to the side of the Up siding has been repaired and the height increased since we last visited this location.

CLIMBING TO WHITEBALL SUMMIT

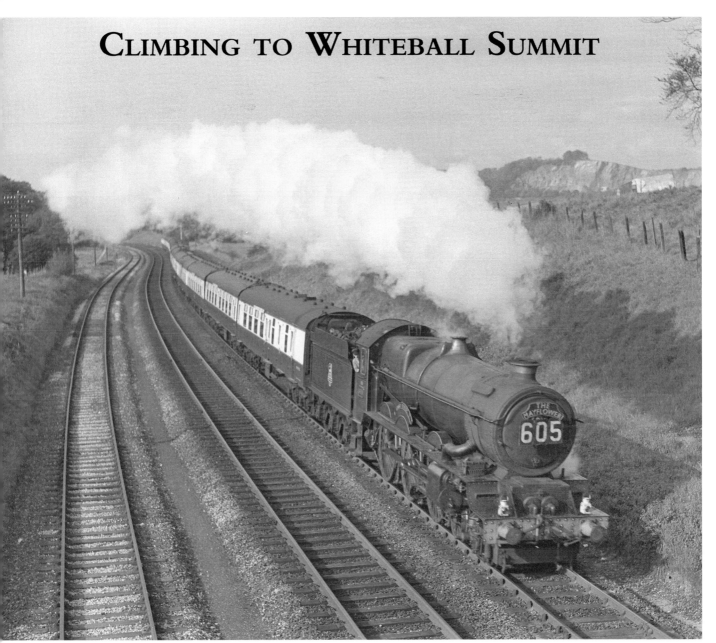

ABOVE: A 'King' Class 4-6-0 (number not recorded but it looks to be No. 6019 *King Henry V*) climbs towards the summit at Whiteball Tunnel with an Up working of 'The Mayflower', complete with a set of BR Mk coaches in chocolate & cream livery and with roof boards. The train was named after the famous 17th century ship that carried the Pilgrim Fathers from England to Plymouth, Massachusetts in 1620. Most likely this photograph was taken on the same day as that on the previous page. On 20th April 1957, the Mayflower II, *built at Brixham as a replica of the original ship, set sail for America from Plymouth amidst great publicity. Doubtless, this was the event which prompted the WR to name the 8.30am Plymouth-Paddington and 5.30pm return as 'The Mayflower'. Looking at the WR Public Time table for summer 1957, the new title was not shown; perhaps it was introduced too late to be included before the document was printed (or was overlooked!). It first appeared 'in print', therefore, in the winter time table applicable from 16th September 1957.*

RIGHT: In contrast to the main photograph, Class '2884' 2-8-0 No. 3864 makes a more measured climb with a train of coal empties comprising wagons of both wooden and steel construction. The driver can be seen through the front spectacle window of the cab – he had spotted Norman with his camera. No rear end banker was required for a load of this tonnage. *22nd April 1957*

THE WARREN & SEA WALL

Norman took only two photographs featuring Western Region steam at Exeter – one at Cowley Bridge, the other at St. Davids. Both had appeared before so we jump now to the southern end of the Exe Estuary at Dawlish Warren, before visiting the sea wall east of Dawlish. No. 7031 *Cromwell's Castle* has a clear road through Dawlish Warren station with the 1.30pm Paddington-Penzance, here loaded to 11 coaches. This was a service which ran non-stop between Exeter and Newton Abbot, at which place the rear coaches would be taken off to proceed, at 5.35pm, all stations to Kingswear. *21st June 1955*
To the left a 'Camping Coach' has been stabled for the 1955 summer season. Such facilities still exist here in 2011 but standing on isolated lengths of rail track. It must have been a day of settled weather because somebody has hung out a towel or cloth to dry!

Dawlish before the summer crowd arrive. This is the view looking wes towards Dawlish station, adjacen to the Rockstone footbridge, which crosses the line and provides access to the sea wall high level footpath. The latter extends eastwards from here to the Langstone Rock. The shadow of a clean exhaust, created in the bright sunshine, is cast across the cliff face as No. 5059 *Earl St Aldwyn*, in charge of the 9.20am local stopping service from Kingswear to Exeter St. Davids regains speed after departing Dawlish at 10.32am. Notice Norman's camera case on top of the wall dividing the footway from the railway and how a little to the west, this section of the high level footway comes to an end *16th April 1955*
No. 5059 had entered service in June 1937 as Powis Castle. *Just a few months later, this locomotive was one of twenty-one (No's 5043 to 5063) which took the names that, earlier the same year, had initially been allocated to the 'Earl' Class 4-4-0s.*

Right on cue, a resplendent No. 6009 *King Charles II* (81A) heads the 6.25am Penzance to Paddington away from its call at Exeter St. Davids. *16th April 1957 This service was booked to commence from Penzance with just three coaches in tow (Van Second, Second, Composite) and collected another five (including an ex-GWR Dining car) at Plymouth. The make-up of the stock seen here is not 'as booked' and included, at the front, a Collett large window Second. The sight and sound of a steam locomotive was such an everyday occurrence that the two children were obviously more interested in the activities of the photographer than the passing 'King'!*

'COUNTIES' & TUNNELS

ABOVE: Dwarfed by the cliff face at Coryton Cove, immaculate No. 1016 *County of Hants* is caught in the sunshine of springtime morning between Coryton and Kennaway Tunnels. Shrewsbury-based No. 1016 had returned from a General Repair at Swindon only a month earlier. The train was the 8.0am Plymouth to Liverpool express, which included portion for Manchester and Glasgow. At the rear of the train (here still to emerge from Coryton Tunnel) a portion from Kingswear had been added at Newton Abbot. Hence the varied stock which included (from the front) an ex-LM&SR Stanier Period II an ex-L&NWR 'toplight', followed by Collett, Hawksworth and BR examples. *16th April 1957*

This one has appeared before; possibly Norman submitted it to the Ian Allen organisation because, many years later, it appeare in one of their books! David & I also published it previously but this is the first time the entire image has been included so the the train can be seen in the full context of the dramatic surroundings. In 2007, award winning, locally-based, railway artist Joh Austin, who has created several superb paintings featuring the sea wall section, completed a wonderful canvas depicting the vie at Coryton Cove but including a wider vista than that photographed here by Norman a half century earlier.

INSET LEFT & BELOW: The 'County' Class, as listed in the Ian Allan 'abc' for 1950 and the list of tunnels between Dawlish an Teignmouth, taken from the GWR *General Appendix to the Rule Book*, 1st August 1936.

LIST OF TUNNELS (2 CHAINS AND OVER IN LENGTH) ON G.W.R. AND ON JOINT LINES.

Name.					No. of lines through.	From		To		Length in Yards.
						Miles.	Chains.	Miles.	Chains.	
Kennaway	...	...	...	...	2	206	34	206	43¼	209
Coryton	...	...	...	...	2	206	52½	206	63	231
Phillot	...	...	...	...	2	206	66¼	206	68¾	55
Clerk's	...	...	...	...	2	206	72	206	75	66
Parson's	...	...	...	...	2	207	18¾	207	42	512

Later the same morning, Norman transferred his attention from Coryton Cove to the eastern end of the seawall section leading from Teignmouth, here near the bottom of Smugglers Lane in Holcombe. During the mid to late 1950s, this had become one of his favourite locations on the South Devon coastline. At 12.35pm, another example of Hawksworth's 4-6-0s, No. 1009 *County of Carmarthen*, emerged from the western portal of Parsons Tunnel, the most westerly of the five tunnels between this point and Dawlish. No. 1009 had charge of the 7.30am Paddington-Paignton which ran the 'Great Way Round', via Bath and Bristol. Hence, the 9.30pm from Paddington (via Castle Cary) would be less than 20 mins behind the 7.30am at this stage in their respective journeys! *16th April 1957* No. 1009 was a Bath Road allocation and had paid two recent visits to Swindon – from 7/8/56 to 19/9/56 for Heavy Intermediate repair, and 16/11/57 to 24/1/57 for an Unclassified repair. From whatever angle these locomotives were observed, in this writer's opinion they were not, by any means, attractive machines when compared with the earlier designs of Churchward and Collett. Notice, by the way, the 'pill-box' built against the rock face adjacent to the tunnel portal – shades of Capt. Mainwaring et al.

6018 WITH '608'

My justification for including another 'two-pager' featuring the sea wall section is that 1958 heralded the appearance of the first of the new 'breed' of diesel-hydraulic locomotives on this route, an event which would lead to the transfer of the 'King' Class away from the West Country and, all too soon, the elimination of steam from the Western Region. The view above is looking westwards between Parson's Tunnel and Sprey Point. No. 6018 *King Henry VI* has the 6.25am Penzance-Paddington running exactly to time – 10.52 am off Teignmouth and here 2 to 3 mins later, as noted by Norman, on the approach to Parson's Tunnel. *26th June 1958*

As is evident from its appearance, No. 6018 had only recently returned into service (allocated to 81A) following a Heavy Intermediate overhaul at Swindon (22/1/58 – 21/3/58), which included the fitting of a twin blastpipe and double chimney. Notice how, during the steam era, the cliff face was kept much clearer of vegetation than is generally the case nowadays. A few people are enjoying the sea air on their morning stroll along the wall but, being only late June, very few youngsters are venturing to the water's edge. In any case, this section of the beach is always much less frequented by holidaymakers. The signal – its arm almost lost from view against the background – is the Down Distant for Teignmouth.

PARSON'S TUNNEL

The fireman looks to be enjoying the sea air as he takes a temporary rest from his duties with Taunton based No. 4971 *Stanway Hall*, heading a westbound Class 'H' freight into the mid-day sunshine.
30th September 1959

I had thought the bicycle parked near the foot of the cliffs on the Up side of the line might belong to the local signalman. However, this was a Wednesday and with the summer season over for another year, it was most unlikely Parson's Tunnel box (just out of view to the left of this scene) was 'switched in'. On a sunny day it must have proved a wonderful place to work – the box usually open as a 'break section' for one turn only on Saturdays during the height of the season. In any case, I have just noticed – the bike is a ladies model!

ABOVE: Nearly 2½ hours after taking the picture opposite, Newton Abbot's 2-6-2T No. 5150 (83A) emerged from the tunnel with the 2.15pm Exeter-Kingswear. During the period of the winter time table, this service conveyed, from St. David's station, the Torbay and Kingswear coaches from the Down 'Cornishman'. The three BR Mk 1 coaches in their chocolate & cream livery are seen tacked on at the rear of this local, which also called at Dawlish and Teignmouth. *30th September 1959*
I recall reading somewhere in the distant past that the railway's private water supply at Newton Abbot was sometimes contaminated, which caused locomotives allocated at 83A to prime. That might explain the condition of No. 5150 as caught here by Norman!

RIGHT: At exactly 12 noon, 'Battle of Britain' Class No. 34060 *25 Squadron*, of Exmouth Junction (72A), heads the 11.25am Exeter-Newton Abbot stopping train, which continued from there as the 12.30pm to Plymouth North Road. *28th September 1957*
The appearance of a Southern Region locomotive (invariably a Bulleid 'Light Pacific' during the late 1950s) was a four times a day occurrence. This was a reciprocal agreement which reached back to GWR/ Southern Railway days, that enabled enginemen to establish and maintain knowledge of the alternative routes linking Exeter and Plymouth should either be temporarily closed to through traffic. Judging from Norman's photograph, the days when both companies invariably put a highly polished engine on their rival's line when working these services had long since passed.

EAST & WEST OF TEIGNMOUTH

Despite the lack of information (David found this one with another small number of plates which included very few details), I included this shot because it shows how close the management of the Western Region of BR came to recreating the image of the former GWR in the latter years of the 1950s. Under heavy enlargement of the scan, the engine can be seen to be No. 6017 *King Edward IV*.

Identification of the locomotive strengthens my thoughts that this picture must have been taken during summer 1957. The 'King' looks as though it has only recently returned from a visit to Swindon Works and the Engine History Sheet reveals that No. 6017 received a Heavy Intermediate repair between 29/4/57 and 18/6/57. John Lewis does not have the details of the usual formation of train No. 605 (the 8.30am Plymouth-Paddington) for the summer of 1957. However, he has been able to provide details for winter 1956-7, which look to be much the same as seen here. Some of the stock listed as 'Fridays Only' is not present in the picture, which rules out the photograph having been taken on that day of the week. Otherwise the formation comprises as follows: Van Second, Second, and Compo. (a three-coach portion ex-8.45am Paignton). Next follow a Van Second, First, Kitchen First, Second Dining Saloon, Second and another Van Second. These were all Plymouth to Paddington. All were BR Mk1 coaches except for the kitchen-diner set, which were ex-GWR painted to match the brown & cream livery of the Mk 1 stock. There are three further coaches bringing up the rear; coach 10 is almost certainly also in brown & cream whilst the last two are most likely in crimson & cream. As the slip portion for this service was still running, these may both be destined for Reading or one for Paddington with a single slip for Reading. The return working for the stock was the 5.30pm from Paddington, except for the slip coach which returned to Plymouth on the 3.28pm Reading (2.30pm ex-Paddington) parcels train. The slip had ceased running by the autumn of 1958, by which date this service ran as 'The Mayflower'. Apparently, the WR Restaurant car department much preferred the ex-GWR cars to newer BR Mk1 examples, which is why some of the former (as per the example here) were painted in BR brown & cream.

The signal opposite the rear of the train was the Teignmouth Down Home which, as can be seen, was in a very exposed location. This section of the line being subject to flooding, the track circuit controlling this signal was likely to fail which, in turn, prevented the signal arm being cleared for the passage of a train. A telephone connected to Teignmouth Signal Box was provided and, in the event of a train being brought to a stand at this signal, the fireman had to communicate with the signalman. If the signal was unable to be lowered because of failure of the track circuit or other apparatus, the signalman would instruct the fireman when it was safe to pass the signal at danger. The full instructions (as contained in the 'Sectional Appendix' for the Exeter Traffic District) were rather more comprehensive than space here permits for repetition, especially when the signal box at Dawlish was switched out.

If you were photographing from the other side of Shaldon Bridge, you might just make it back to here with your trousers rolled up before a fast-incoming tide fills the Teign Estuary! This is the scene looking due west on the north side of the estuary, near a location known locally as 'Polly Steps', near the western end of Teignmouth Docks. No. 6010 *King Charles I* approaches with the 9.20am (SO) St. Ives-Paddington. Norman described the train as the 'Up relief *Riviera*'; a reference to the fact that whilst, on weekdays, the 'CRE' included a portion from St. Ives, on summer Saturdays this was expanded into a separate through train from the seaside resort, which left St. Erth at 9.40am and ran ahead of the main 'CRE', arriving at Paddington (scheduled as non-stop from Plymouth) at 4.40pm.

25th June 1955

As mentioned on the full title page, the start of the summer 1955 time table had been deferred as a consequence of the ASLEF strike so, officially at least, the summer workings did not commence until the Monday following this visit by Norman to the lineside. Evidently, however, with the strike settled, here already were summer Saturday trains at work.

SHALDON BRIDGE – 2

ABOVE: Norman has moved a little farther onto the bridge to obtain this wider view of the approach of the railway from the Newton Abbot direction. The Teign estuary is in full flood, as No. 5021 *Whittington Castle* (a Laira-based locomotive) approaches Teignmouth with the 9.30am (SX) Falmouth to Paddington. After making a few calls on the run up through Cornwall, this service was scheduled non-stop from Plymouth (where a Restaurant car was added) arriving at Paddington at 4.20pm. Norman recorded the time as 1.05pm, so with a scheduled departure from North Road exactly an hour earlier, the train was running to time. *26th June 1958*
The buildings just visible squeezed between the railway and the river had formed a part of the Teignmouth Gas Works which had been closed in the mid 1950s and the site sold into private ownership. When still in use as a gas works, it was served by a single siding controlled from a ground frame.

LEFT: BR 'Britania' Class 4-6-2 No. 70019 *Lightning* (allocated to Laira) was recorded by Norman at 3.30pm which meant the 10.50am (Sundays) Paddington-Paignton was almost 20 minutes down on schedule. This service – non-stop to Exeter, then Dawlish and all stations (Kingskerswell excepted) to Paignton – was scheduled to run on only four consecutive Sundays at the height of the holiday season, this being the last in 1955. *28th August 1955*
Note the poor external appearance of No. 70019 compared with the Canton-based locomotives of this class as seen elsewhere in this book. Rumour had it they were not well received at Laira.

KINGSKERSWELL

A favourite of Newton Abbot shed for this service, No. 5078 *Beaufort* approaches Kingskerswell with the Down 'Torbay Express', the 12 noon Paddington-Kingswear. Norman is standing on the overbridge immediately to the north of Kingskerswell station which, until closure on 5th October 1964, was the first station beyond Newton Abbot on the line to Kingswear. *26th June 1958*

Notice the Up Starting signal in the foreground, shortened and repositioned in January 1941 to provide easier sighting under the road bridge for approaching trains. Nowadays, the view over the parapet of this bridge is much restricted by tree growth and barely recognisable to that seen above. 'Dobbins Arch', the overbridge seen in the background, is now a Grade II Listed structure, attributed to Brunel and the South Devon Railway. No. 5078, which had entered service in May 1939 as Lamphey Castle, was renamed Beaufort in January 1941. Allocated to Newton Abbot since January 1942, this long association was about to be broken when, a month after being photographed here by Norman, the locomotive was transferred to Canton. Inclusion of the full width of Norman's photograph resulted in this scene being spoilt by a very prominent diagonal wire carrying the electricity feed to the lamp of the Up Starting signal. That must have been the reason why, when making a print, Norman chose a format which omitted most of the wire and, in doing so, trimmed out most of the left background. I wished to include the cottages (in Church End Road) as, nowadays, these are the only lineside feature you might recognise of this same view (albeit they are now surrounded by the Kingskerswell Parish Centre). So – as will be evident – I must own up to having digitally removed the diagonal wire!

SEVERN TUNNEL JUNCTION

RIGHT: A Sunday visit to Severn Tunnel Junction included a look around the busy motive power depot (86E), which was located on the Up side of the line beyond the eastern end of the station. In 1959, around sixty-six locomotives where allocated here, mostly for goods, shunting and banking duties, including 0-6-2T No. 5679. The lined green livery was first applied to this class during 1957, so No. 5679 must have received this on her last visit to Swindon (24/9/58 to 29/10/58) for a Heavy Intermediate repair. *If nothing else, this photograph is proof that photographers, even those as gifted as Norman, occasionally made mistakes, here with the consequence that the telegraph pole in the background appears to be emerging from the safety bonnet of the 0-6-2T! David suggests that his father would not have made a print from this plate.*

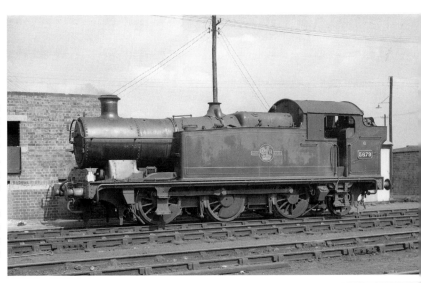

ABOVE: 0-6-0T No. 2231 was standing outside the eastern end of the mpd, on one of the two additional through shed roads provided when the depot was extended in 1931. Eleven years had passed since the demise of the GWR but the company roundel is still displayed on the tender side. Standing in front of it, Collett 0-6-2T No. 6672 has various messages chalked up either side of the cab doorway: '*Eng Prep 29 Aug Keep Off*' must have made sense to somebody whilst '*No fire 29/8*' left nothing to the imagination! Almost hidden from view inside the shed is 2-8-0 No. 2873. All three locomotives were based here.

LEFT: WD 2-8-0 No. 90433 was a visitor from Woodford Halse (2F), with the front end of another member of the same class, No. 90299 just visible behind.

No. 90433 had been one of the 2-8-0s ordered by the Ministry of Supply for the WD, built by the Vulcan Foundry at Newton-le-Willows numbered WD7473 and released into traffic in January 1944. The numbers of these engines were given an additional digit from Sept 1944 the above example becoming WD77473. It was taken into L&NER Book Stock on 28/12/46 and renumbered 3112 in February 1947. The final renumbering to 90433 is recorded as 28/10/50 Withdrawn 25/4/64, this 'Austerity' was sold to Cashmore of Great Bridge and their records show it taken into their yard on 18/9/64.

This is Norman's only photograph to feature the station (or, at least, a part of it), so despite his lack of details, it is worthy of inclusion. Carrying the '719' reporting number, this 'Castle'-hauled express would be the 11.55am (Sundays) Paddington-Pembroke Dock (a 'dated' summer service). Photographed from the overbridge at the west end of the station, the train is passing the northern face of the island platform (No. 3) which serves the Down 'Tunnel Line'. Just west of the station, the lines via the Severn Tunnel merge with those coming in from the Gloucester via Chepstow route, continuing then as four tracks on towards Newport and along which this service is about to travel.

Severn Tunnel Junction today is but a shadow of its former self, with the station buildings all swept away and the footbridge replaced with a more utilitarian metal structure. Four platform faces remain but are now adorned with 'bus shelters'. The vast array of sidings which once existed here have all been lifted and the mpd raised to the ground, although a small compound remains for stabling the Severn Tunnel maintenance train. Situated close to the banks of the Severn estuary, the station is a bleak spot in the depths of winter!

SWINDON

Norman has this as the 1.0pm (the public time table stated 1.20pm) Paddington to Swindon, a train which included a Restaurant car, seen here following arrival at Swindon Junction behind No. 7016 *Chester Castle*. What a Landore based locomotive (87E) was doing on this train can perhaps be explained by a reader with access to the appropriate engine diagram for May 1959. Norman had travelled to Swindon for a Sunday visit to the Works yards. *24th May 1959*

Coincidentally, one of the locomotives Norman photographed at the Works was the member of the class which immediately preceded that seen in the top picture. No. 7015 *Carn Brea Castle* was just out of 'A' Shop following a General Repair, which included the fitting of a twin blastpipe and double chimney. All records show that this locomotive, here coupled to a Collett 4,000 gallon tender, was reallocated (whilst at Swindon) to '84A' – Stafford Road (Wolverhampton), yet here an '84G' (Shrewsbury) shedplate had been affixed! As we have already seen (page 101), it was not unknown for the incorrect shedplate (or smokebox door?) to be fixed following overhaul of an engine at Swindon. *24th May 1959 Coincidentally, after five months based at Stafford Road following this overhaul No. 7015 was reallocated to '84G' during w/e 31/10/59.*

Just out of the erecting shop at Swindon and yet to be 'lit up' for the first time, BR Class '9F' No. 92207 sparkles in the mid-day sunshine. This 2-10-0 was one of the final 'Lot' of steam locomotives to be built at Swindon, culminating just 9½ months later with the completion of No. 92220 *Evening Star*. By this date, Swindon was already building some of the early diesel hydraulic locomotives and the fact that No. 92207 was to remain in traffic for a mere 5 years and 7 months is but one example of why, subsequently, many have questioned the policy of permitting steam locomotive production to continue into the late 1950s. *24th May 1959*

No. 92207 was allocated initially to '82B', Bristol St. Philip's Marsh from 1st June 1959. In February 1960, it was transferred to Southall. From here, some records suggest it moved first to Oxford and then to Banbury but these may have been loans from Southall. No. 92207 was transferred to its final depot, Newport Ebbw Junction, in mid November 1964 and withdrawn the following month. The locomotive was sold to Woodhams in February 1965 and transferred to their Barry scrap yard during the following month. Having lain there, rusting away for 21½ years, No. 92207 was purchased by well-known artist Keith Bottomley, named 'Morning Star', and – during late October 1986 – transported by road to Bury, on the East Lancashire Railway. There it remained for nineteen years, during which time many new parts were acquired and a complete restoration of the main frames, axleboxes and five wheelsets undertaken. During December 2005, the locomotive in its partially restored condition was moved to Shillingstone station, which is the headquarters of the Shillingstone Railway Project under the auspices of the North Dorset Railway Trust.

Yet to be reunited with a tender but looking absolutely spotless in unlined black livery following a Heavy Intermediate repair, '2884' Class No. 3856 (84C) was one of the final batch, built in 1942, during Collett's regime. Other than outside steam pipes, side cab windows and modified frames, these latter engines appeared little modified from Churchward's classic design of 1903. The 'X' painted under the 'E' Group classification on the cab side indicated the locomotive was permitted to haul loads over the maximum otherwise permitted for this Group. *24th May 1959*

On another Sunday visit, Norman found this line-up outside the running shed. 'Castle' Class No. 5058 *Earl of Clancarty* keeps company with BR Class '9F' 2-10-0 No. 92210 and ex-L&NER Class 'B1' 4-6-0 No. 61106, the latter probably having worked into Swindon, via Banbury, with a train from Woodford Halse. In the right background, another Class '9F', No. 92212, is lurking. Both of these 2-10-0s had been built at Swindon during 1957. *27th September 1959*

LEFT: Also just outshopped in unlined black livery following a 'Heavy' Intermediate repair (recorded as 12/9/60 to 11/11/60), Churchward 2-8-0T No. 4272, carrying an 87F (Llanelly) shedplate, looks resplendent with the low Winter sun picking out her 'below footplate' details. Norman noted the date as 6th November 1960, so prior to No. 4272 being 'run in' before returning to her home shed. Less than three years later, she was withdrawn from Cardiff East Dock mpd during w/e 12/10/63 and sold to Hayes of Bridgend on 1/1/64.

BELOW: A line of five locomotives which had been overhauled standing alongside 'J' Shop, each waiting to be united with a tender. From the front, we have No. 6915 *Mursley Hall* (81E), No. 4963 *Rignall Hall* (84B), 2-8-0 No. 3823 (81F), No. 6935 *Browsholme Hall* (86C) and – bringing up the rear – No. 7901 *Dodington Hall* (82A). Each, except No. 6915, had received a General Repair, the exception having undergone a Heavy Intermediate repair. *27th September 1959*

ABOVE: A scene inside the 'A' Erecting Shop. This being a Sunday, the scene bears little relation to the bustle (and noise!) encountered on working days. Centre of attraction is Churchward 2-8-0 No. 4700. Records state it was sent to Works on 26/8/59 and out again on 20/11/59. As will be noted, the livery is fully lined green. Numerals chalked on the boiler backplate and firehole shelfplate of the adjacent locomotive (to the right) reveal it to be No. 6942 *Eshton Hall* and records confirm this 4-6-0 was in the Works from 9/10/59 to 18/11/59. The two engines were allocated to Old Oak Common and both were in the Shop for a General Repair. *8th November 1959*
Mention of the practice of chalking numbers on various parts of a locomotive taken apart for repair brings back happy memories of the writer's own visits to Swindon on Wednesday afternoons during the 1950s, when production of your rail ticket gained you entry for a conducted tour of the Works. I recollect arguments with one or two fellow 'locospotters' who, on seeing – for example – a row of chimneys laid out along a shop floor and each bearing the chalked number of the engine to which they were to be reunited, promptly claimed each as a 'cop' irrespective of whether they actually saw those locomotives during the processional walk around the site!

OPPOSITE PAGE TOP: This third visit during 1959 was again blessed with fine weather. Looking absolutely immaculate in fully lined green livery following a General Repair, No. 4905 waits to be reunited with a tender and 'run-in' before returning to her allocated shed at Newton Abbot (83A). No. 4905 *Barton Hall* was constructed at Swindon in 1928, one of the first of these two-cylinder mixed traffic locomotives of a design which continued, with modification, until 1950, when the last was rolled out of Swindon Works. *8th November 1959*.

OPPOSITE PAGE BOTTOM: No. 6016 *King Edward V* looks equally as impressive having transferred to the motive power depot at Swindon following a General Repair in the Works. Now the locomotive will be 'run-in' on a series of local turns, before returning to Old Oak Common to resume top link duties. Tucked away in the right background are No. 5002 *Ludlow Castle* and an 0-6-0 BR diesel shunter. *8th November 1959*
Note the chalked message on the smokebox door – presumably a reminder that the front screens to the self cleaning cage inside the smokebox needed to be secured. The double chimney and twin orifice blastpipe had been modifications undertaken during an earlier visit to the Works in 1956.

CLEVEDON BRANCH

Although close to his home town of Weston-super-Mare, it was not until after Norman had moved to Bath that he photographed the 3½ mile branch line from Yatton to Clevedon, on several occasions during the late 1950s. His last visit in August 1960 was the final day when this line was operated by the Collett auto-fitted 0-4-2Ts. From Monday 8th August 1960, the passenger services were taken over by diesel multiple units and these continued in use until the last trains ran on Saturday 1st October 1966.

ABOVE: The polished lined-green livery gleams in the evening sunlight as No. 1412 sets off from the Up bay platform at Yatton for the 7 minute scheduled run to the terminus at Clevedon. Despite this being a Sunday in May, no less than thirteen return runs would be made and although Norman's photograph shows the 7.03pm departure, there would be another three round trips before No. 1412 was put away for the night. *25th May 1959*

LEFT: The 3.15pm (Sundays) from Yatton to Clevedon must have been running a little late when photographed here by Norman who recorded the time as 3.35pm. No. 1426 was in charge on this occasion. Note the driver's oiling can placed between the smokebox saddle and the back of the leading wheel splasher. At least two passengers are visible in the auto coach – one, in a 'Non Smoking' compartment, who has spotted Norman with his camera, whilst the other might be 'nodding off', although the journey was barely long enough for a nap! *10th July 1960*

ABOVE: No. 1426 pulls away from Yatton with a delayed 6.30pm (Sundays) service to Clevedon. Note the large signal box in the right background, a survivor from the days of the original Bristol & Exeter Railway. The stone building just poking into the left side of this scene is the small shed which housed the branch locomotive. Yatton also served as the junction for the Cheddar Valley line. *10th July 1960*

RIGHT: The following month, Norman returned with Ivo to photograph the branch line train on the final day of steam working. No. 1463 'did the honours', here propelling the 3.58pm Clevedon to Yatton. The driver must have made this journey many hundreds of times; one way in the cab, the other – as seen here – in the leading compartment of the auto trailer. *7th August 1960*
The leading trailer (W233W) was one of those built at Swindon as late as August 1951. The coach (W252W) nearest the engine was also a Driving Trailer but converted from a Brake Third in August 1955. The design had a single large window positioned centrally at one end.

Mid afternoon sunshine during a day in early March illuminates No 7927 *Willington Hall* with the 12.50pm Cardiff-Brighton service. The location is south of Old Dilton, towards the end of the climb from Westbury, through Dilton Marsh, towards Warminster. The Distant signal was controlled by Upton Scudamore Signal Box, which marked the summit of a climb which sometimes demanded an assisting engine for passenger traffic or, more often, a 'banker' for the heavy freight traffic which passed via this important cross-country route. *4th March 1961*

The upper quadrant signal is a consequence of operating control of this former GWR line between Westbury (excluded) to Salisbury passing into the control of the Southern Region from 2nd April 1950. Notice the new system of Four Character Train Identification as introduced with the commencement of the summer time table on 13th June 1960. Steam hauled trains still displayed the class of train by means of their headlamps and retained the use of the three character frames on which were displayed (using a letter followed by two numerals) the destination and identification of the individual train. Thus, we have train number '1O61' – the initial digit being 'Class 1' (replacing the former Class 'A' head code) and the 'O' representing an inter-regional train destined for the Southern Region.

THE 1960s

You may have noticed from the past few pages that we have reached the 1960s. What is very evident from the notebooks containing Norman's photographic records is just how quickly – as the early 'sixties' progressed – his output of photographs featuring main line Western Region steam diminished. Whilst, of course, this was a direct consequence of the increasing use of diesel hydraulic motive power, it is also obvious that he was now concentrating on making more visits to those areas where steam still reigned (more or less) supreme for just a few more years. Trips to the lineside on the Western Region tended to focus a little more on the increasing number of 'specials' – whether they were 'last day' events or the last (or near-last) running of a specific locomotive. The few ex-GWR main lines that remained as a bastion of steam-hauled motive power for a few more years, included the Gloucester-Paddington and Worcester-Paddington routes to which Norman, often in the company of Ivo Peters, paid due homage. What is also noticeable is the fact that, whereas most of his lineside visits in earlier years enjoyed fine weather, those undertaken as the 'Swinging Sixties' progressed were – more often than not – bedevilled by less favourable conditions.

Canton-based No. 5099 *Compton Castle* **is being worked hard on the 1 in 70 climb with the 1.0pm Cardiff-Brighton. Having regard to the date recorded by Norman, the autumn that year must have remained mild (even by the conditions we usually enjoy here in West Wiltshire), because the trees in the background were still showing their foliage – doubtless by this late date in hues of orange and brown. Many were elms, a species which would later suffer from the dreaded 'Dutch Elm' disease, that would wipe huge numbers of these fine trees from the landscape. No. 5099 was resplendent in the mid afternoon sunshine, having received a General Repair at Swindon during May/June that year.** *4th November 1961*
This photograph caused me some grief! I had queried the accuracy of the locomotive number as recorded by Norman because, if it was as claimed, then why was it carrying a Cathays shedplate when records showed it allocated to Canton? It was Richard Strange who subsequently reminded me that, at the start of 1960, certain changes were made to the shed codes and the Cathays code (88A) was reallocated to Canton depot!

UPTON SCUDAMORE

In stark contrast to the photograph on page 138, here No. 7927 *Willington Hall* was in a poor external state of cleanliness, which seems to mirror the lighting conditions. The number/name of the 'Modified Hall' were unrecorded at the time by Norman but the locomotive has been identified half a century later thanks to digital manipulation of the image. The fact that it is definitely No. 7927 came as a surprise; just look how much the external condition of this engine had deteriorated within less than three months. This is again the 1.0pm Cardiff to Brighton train, here just a little farther south and heading through the cutting leading to the summit of the 2½mile climb near Upton Scudamore. The Canton-based 4-6-0 has assistance provided by 0-6-2T No. 5689, a long-term allocation to Westbury where, doubtless, the tank engine will have been attached to this train for the ascent of the stiff climb. *20th May 1961*

The allocation of motive power at Westbury (82D) included two (sometimes three) of the Collett mixed class 0-6-2Ts. Their main duties were banking the heavy coal and other freight traffic between Westbury and Upton Scudamore. When the box at the head of the incline was 'switched out' or when coupled 'inside', as here, to a passenger service, the 0-6-2T worked through to Warminster – the next block post, around another 2 miles to the south – before returning, light engine, to Westbury.

Why the words 'Do not bump' were chalked on the buffer plank over the front right hand buffer (as viewed) of the leading locomotive must remain a mystery. Notice the cylinder casing also bears a chalk inscription. All of this might appear to suggest that No. 7927 had recently been 'in Works' but the previous such recorded visit was a General Repair at Swindon nine months earlier (4/8/60 to 16/9/60). So, more likely, the 'Do not bump' was written whilst the locomotive was stored on a shed road with the cylinder casing removed and/or some minor work undertaken. Having been out of action might also explain the deterioration in the state of cleanliness, with No. 7927 perhaps being press-ganged back into action at short notice before receiving any attention from an oily rag!

As mentioned a couple of pages ago, this route was an important cross country link. Travelling the line nowadays, it is difficult to envisage how much coal and freight traffic travelled between South Wales and the South Coast, via Bristol and Salisbury, more than half-a-century ago. Somehow a regular service of Class 158 DMU 'Sprinters' does not hold quite the same fascination! Still, it is a route which witnesses the passage of main line steam tours on a fairly regular basis.

NORTON BAVANT

A Sunday afternoon visit to the lineside near Norton Bavant, south of Warminster, found (what we believe to be) No. 6936 *Breccles Hall* with the 2.15pm (Sundays) Portsmouth-Cardiff inter-regional working. This same scene was photographed by Ivo Peters who, most out of character, also overlooked recording details of the motive power! I can imagine a conversation along the following lines: *"Well, what was the number and name, Norman?"* – *"But I thought you were making a note, Ivo!"* 20th March 1960

Norton Bavant village lies close to this line which traverses the picturesque Wylye Valley to Wilton, to the north of Salisbury. The train photographed here by Norman was subject to one of those time table quirks which must have had some unrecorded historical significance, in that it called at the little halt at Dilton Marsh yet sped through the town of Bradford-on-Avon without pausing for custom! This, of course, was before Sir John Betjeman immortalised 'Dilton Marsh Halt' in his poem bearing that title!

A Touch of Spendour for a Sad Event

In 1960, the last steam locomotive built for British Railways was constructed at Swindon – BR Class '9F' 2-10-0 No. 92220, which was to be named *Evening Star*. As part of the naming ceremony for the engine, these two famous elderly locomotives, GWR 4-4-0 No. 3440 *City of Truro* and Caledonian Railway 'Single' No. 123, were placed on display inside the 'A' Shop in the Works at Swindon. Two days later they were pulled out of the works prior to transfer to the stock shed, a task allocated to an 0-6-0 pannier tank, the external condition of which contrasted somewhat markedly with the two veterans. A few days later, both locomotives ran under their own steam to Bristol where they were put on public display at Temple Meads, before travelling on to Cardiff for a similar event. *20th March 1960*

Norman found No. 92220 in the yard at Swindon but, unfortunately, not in the most photogenic location, even within the environs of a railway works! Rather appropriately, Swindon had given the engine a copper-capped chimney and turned it out in a standard green fully lined livery. The name *Evening Star* had been revealed at an official ceremony which took place inside the famous Swindon 'A' shop on Friday 18th March 1960. *20th March 1960*
Norman photographed this same scene in 35mm colour and the shot included the top of a large stack of timber which appeared over the top of the boiler. However, the offending stack has 'vanished' from the scan made from his glass plate negative taken using his quarter-plate press camera! I hope the purists will not object.

A study of chimneys! Another visit to Swindon later in 1960 found this line-up of locomotives reunited with tenders following overhaul. From right to left are 'Castle' No. 7001 *Sir James Milne* (which had received a General Repair and was allocated to Old Oak Common), No. 1026 *County of Salop* (Heavy Intermediate Repair and allocated to Shrewsbury) and No. 5021 *Whittingham Castle* (General Repair and reallocated to SPM, then to Canton). During the overhaul, No. 7001 (originally named *Denbigh Castle* but renamed in 1948 in recognition of the last General Manager of the GWR), received a twin blastpipe and double chimney. The squat double chimney sported by No. 1026 dated from an earlier Works visit (9/5/58 to 31/10/58), whilst No. 5021 retained the original single chimney. *11th September 1960*
No. 5021 had come to Swindon as a locomotive allocated to Bath Road. However, whilst 'in the shops' (27/6/60 to 15/9/60), Bath Road was closed as a steam shed, so the locomotive was returned initially to St. Philip's Marsh then transferred to Canton.

NEWPORT

In a condition befitting this top-link turn worked by a Canton locomotive, Britannia Pacific No. 70027 *Rising Star* restarts 'The Red Dragon' from Newport High Street station. This was the 7.30am from Carmarthen to Paddington which No. 70027 took over at Cardiff for a 10.0am departure. Norman logged the time of his photograph as 10.20am, so the express was 'right time' as it regained the Up main line from Platform 5. In the background, a '42XX' 2-8-0T waits for a clear line with a Class 'H' freight, the front wagons loaded with sawn timber. *20th June 1960* No. 70027 was allocated to Canton (on 24/10/52) from new and remained there until transferred to the LMR on 11/9/61. Notice the 'hand-holds' cut into the deflector plates. This modification was a replacement for the original handrails, the positioning of which were found to partially obscure forward vision from the footplate. This matter had been considered a contributory factor leading to the first serious accident to involve one of these locomotives, during November 1955. No. 70026 *Polar Star* – at the head of an excursion train – had been driven through a crossover at excessive speed, derailed and rolled down an embankment, overturning some of the coaches behind and resulting in 11 fatalities and injuries to 157 passengers.

RIGHT: Norman took just this one photograph looking almost south from the Cardiff end of the station. At 7.15pm, No. 4094 *Dynevor Castle* emerges into bright sunshine after passing through Hillfield Tunnel and under Bridge Road overbridge. The locomotive, an allocation to Landore, had only recently returned from a Heavy Intermediate repair at Swindon (1/1/60 to 29/3/60). The painted buffers were a trademark of Landore shed, which invariably maintained its fleet of 'namers' in superb condition (although in this instance the cleaning did not appear to include the tender). *20th June 1960*
The train is the 2.30pm Neyland-Paddington, a stopping train as far as Swansea, then Neath, Port Talbot, Bridgend and Cardiff to Newport. Arrival here was scheduled for 7.17pm. From Newport, the train was scheduled non-stop to Swindon, calling then only at Reading before reaching Paddington.

BELOW: Another Landore-based 4-6-0, No. 7028 *Cadbury Castle*, waits time at Platform 6 with the Down 'South Wales Pullman' – by this date timed as the 8.50am departure from Paddington with a scheduled non-stop run to Newport. This Pullman service worked as far west as Swansea, returning from there as the 4.30pm departure. Notice the steward suitably attired, although patronage at Newport appeared somewhat sparse on this occasion. As from 11th September 1961, the steam hauled service was replaced by a Metro-Cammell 'Blue Pullman' set. *24th April 1961*
Note the freight passing on the Up Main line under the authority of the small 'Calling On' signal. I wonder to which locomotive the boiler/firebox seen on the bogie bolster wagon had last belonged?

The 8.0am Neyland-Paddington (also conveying through coaches from Fishguard Harbour and from Pembroke Dock) is restarted from Newport by No. 6003 *King George IV*. During 1961, several of the 'Kings' had been allocated to Canton shed as the consequence of their being displaced from duties to and from the West Country. Soon, however, the ever burgeoning stock of main line diesel-hydraulic locomotives would make the 'Kings' redundant on the South Wales traffic as well. The entire class was withdrawn during 1962, No. 6003 from Canton in June that year – just nine months after being photographed here by Norman. *18th September 1961*

'Drinka Pinta Milka Day' – the slogan introduced in 1958 by the National Milk Publicity Council. It was probably one of the best remembered advertising slogans dating from the late 1950s/early '60s. A decade later, 'Margaret Thatcher – Milk Snatcher' appeared when, as Education Secretary of State in 1971, she decided to end free school milk for children over seven years of age!

Churchward 2-8-0T No. 4276 trundles westwards through the station with a train of mineral empties, passing No. 5073 *Blenheim* waiting, light engine, near the end of Platform 5. The 2-8-0 was based at Newport Pill (86B). The 4-6-0 had transferred from Taunton (83B) to Canton just a week previously and had not yet been fitted with an '88A' shed plate. Within a month it would be called to Swindon for a final Heavy Intermediate repair. Note also the two 0-6-0 pannier tanks; one on the extreme left with stock doubtless for a Valleys service whilst, extreme right, the very front of the Newport pilot can be glimpsed, attached to its Shunter's Truck, a once familiar feature. *18th September 1961*

In the spring of 1961, the platforms at Newport were renumbered in conjunction with a revised layout of running lines and a major scheme to install multiple-aspect signalling. In the above view, No. 4376 has just passed under a new MAS gantry. Note also, in the right background, the insulated container van being prepared for transfer to a road trailer. Doubtless, nowadays, 'Health & Safety' would have something to say about an operative standing on top of the container! The major Goods Depot at High Street was closed in the early 1970s.

In late June 1961, Norman paid another brief visit to Hereford. Using the overbridge at the southern end of the (former Barrs Court) station, he took only two photographs. This is the second, which incorporates the trains from both! At 2.40pm, Shrewsbury's No. 7025 *Sudeley Castle* pulls away with the 1.12pm (Sundays) Shrewsbury-Cardiff. No. 7017 *G.J. Churchward* (81A), which arrived earlier with a train from Paddington, had drawn forward and reversed the empty stock into the middle road. To the right, a DMU (a three-car cross country set?) complete with a buffet trailer is stabled waiting the next turn of duty. Note the triple disc ground signals and the single slip points in the foreground. *25th June 1961.*

Notice, as we have progressed through the late 1950s and into the early '60s, how the appearance of the lined maroon livery of the coaching stock has become ever more widely used. As mentioned earlier, this was introduced in 1956 and, as John Lewis reminded me, that was the same year as the WR started using brown & cream coaches for 'titled' train, some of which can be seen amongst the stock behind No. 7017.

A Sunday Afternoon at Hereford

This splendid location was described by Norman as 'near Aberdovey'. Trying to be a little more precise, it has been identified (with the aid of 'Google Earth'?) as between Abertafol Halt and Gogarth Halt on the northern shoreline of the Dovey Estuary, where 2-6-0 No. 6395 is heading the 7.35am from Pwllheli – a part of the 'Cambrian Coast Express'. At Dovey Junction, this portion would be joined with the coaches from Aberystwyth for the continuation, via Welshpool, Shrewsbury (reversal), and Wolverhampton to Paddington. No. 6395 was allocated to Machynlleth (86C), a depot which included a number of sub-sheds including Pwllheli. *30th September 1961*

Apparently it was common practice for additional coaches to be attached to this part of the 'CCE' to cater for local traffic. So I don't know how much of the train seen here might have worked only as far as (for example) Dovey Junction – possibly the last four coaches. However, with the addition of the Aberystwyth portion, at least ten coaches would work forward from Dovey Junction, with the train doubtless double-headed from there to Shrewsbury and with three more coaches added at Wolverhampton.

CAMBRIAN INTERLUDE

In September 1961 Norman accompanied Ivo Peters on a trip to North Wales, primarily to visit the Talyllyn Railway. It proved to be one of several visits to photograph the narrow gauge railways. David and I hope, one day, to add a book to the published *'Norman Lockett Archive'* to feature narrow gauge and industrial railways many of which were photographed by Norman both in monochrome and in colour.

ABOVE: Another delightful scene photographed a half-hour after that seen opposite. Norman and Ivo were able to access the lineside from the nearby main road (A493) which parallels much of this length of the coastal line. BR Class '3MT' 2-6-2T No. 82033 (86C), in lined green livery, is in charge of the 8.40pm Pwllheli-Dovey Junction and is less than 10 minutes from its destination. *30th September 1961*

I find it very disappointing that one of these fine BR 'Standard' 2-6-2Ts did not become the subject of a scheme for preservation. Thankfully, all these years later, this omission is being 'put to rights' with the construction of a brand new member of the class by 'The 82045 Steam Locomotive Trust'. This major project is based at Bridgnorth, on the Severn Valley Railway.

RIGHT: The main purpose for this visit was to photograph (and for Ivo to film) the approach to Towyn of the Talyllyn Railway Preservation Society special train from Paddington, double-headed from Shrewsbury by '45XX' Class 2-6-2T No. 5555 and '22XX' 0-6-0 No. 2222. Seen on the Up side of the main line is the siding and loading dock which had been used for exchange of traffic with the narrow gauge system. Towyn (nowadays the preferred spelling is Tywyn) Wharf is the headquarters of the thriving Talyllyn Railway, a major tourist attraction. *30th September 1961*

No. 2222 was allocated to Shrewsbury (89A). Officially, No. 5555 had been transferred from Shrewsbury to Exeter (83C) during the week ending 9/9/61 but it appears that the locomotive was held back from heading to its new base in order to work this special.

'MIDLAND & SOUTH WESTERN' FAREWELL

ABOVE: Two special trains were run on Sunday, 10th September 1961 to mark the closure (of all but a few short lengths for freight traffic) of the old Midland & South Western Junction Railway route, which linked Andoversford in Gloucestershire with Andover in Hampshire. This had provided a route for through traffic between Cheltenham and Southampton. It was a day of varying weather conditions; sometimes bright periods, at other times cloudy with rain and drizzle. This is the outward journey of the SLS special, which commenced from Birmingham (Snow Hill), with No. 7808 *Cookham Manor* approaching Andoversford on the Cheltenham to Banbury line (which by this date terminated at Rollright Siding, just north of Chipping Norton). To the east of Andoversford station, the special would pass onto the start of the M&SWJR and travel the full length via Cirencester, Swindon, Marlborough and Ludgershall to Red Post Junction, and then to Andover, where No. 7808 was turned for the return journey.

LEFT: The other special was organised by the RCTS, with 2-6-0 No. 5306 as the motive power. This commenced from Swindon Junction (members from London making use of a connecting service) and first ran south to Andover, then northwards over the full length of the M&SWJR to Cheltenham. Norma first photographed the train arriving her at Cirencester (Watermoor) station, where a halt was made so that those wishing could examine the remnants of the former Compan workshops (out of sight to the right), which had closed in 1925. The loop serving the Dow line and all signalling had been taken out of use the previous year. In the right background is Cirencester Gas Works, which was still operational and rail served at this date; closed circa 1964.

Note the deterioration in the weather! No. 5306 was a Pontypool Road allocation at the time of this rail tour.

ABOVE: The wait at Cirencester allowed Norman and Ivo to get ahead of the train to photograph its passage through the remote station of Foss Cross, just south of the summit of the line. With the skies beginning to clear again, No. 5306 enters the loop and passes the signal box, immediately to the rear of which can just be seen the means by which Norman was transported up and down the line that day!

The RCTS Special continued to Cheltenham before returning to Swindon, where London passengers were returned to the Capital by a late-running train. Now 'marooned' in a farmer's field, the brick-built station building at Foss Cross is today one of the few surviving structures of the M&SWJR (apart from some small bridges). The most substantial remaining building is the old three-road engine shed in Cheltenham, which is now in commercial use.

RIGHT: The return run of the SLS Special was photographed at South Cerney (between Cricklade and Cirencester), where the 'Manor' has just drawn to a halt and many of the passengers had 'baled out' only to be shepherded back onto the train. As can be seen here, the train arrived in sunshine but, by the time No. 7808 set off again, northwards to Cheltenham then home to Birmingham, the clouds had closed in once more. This special had made a detour for a brief visit to the Works at Swindon on the return run. Altogether, a good day out for a fare of 25 shillings & 6 pence (£1.27½).

By the way, the 'bits' which give the appearance of sticking out above the cab of No. 7808 are the two ventilators and chimney of the signal box sited on the opposite platform! The signalman, who had just exchanged single line tokens with the fireman, can be seen at the near end of the Up platform.

COALEY JUNCTION

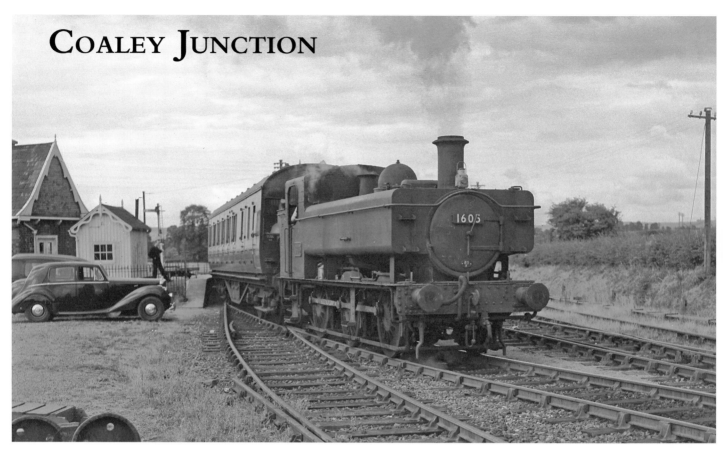

TUFFLEY

NEAR HARESFIELD

ABOVE: I hope this picture proves good enough to publish because the glass plate has deteriorated and requires the skills of our publisher to repair the damage. It represents a scene at the start of the 1960s which would disappear from the Western Region within little more than a few years. Canton-based Collett '2884' Class 2-8-0 No. 3809 trundles towards Standish Junction with a late afternoon train comprised mostly of loaded coal wagons, both steel and wooden bodied examples. *28th May 1960*

Norman didn't record the number of the 2-8-0 but I noticed Ivo (and the top of his Bentley) on the overbridge. A telephone call to Julian Peters and a request that he check Ivo's notes for 28/5/60 quickly brought forward the number of the locomotive. Ivo had taken his photograph of the freight as it approached the bridge from the north. No. 3809 was withdrawn (from Croes Newydd) w/e 24/10/64 and sold to Birds (Morriston) on 14/12/64.

OPPOSITE PAGE TOP: No. 1605 sets off from the sharply curved branch line platform with the 4.42pm Coaley Junction to Dursley, passing what has since become a very well-recognised Bentley. The WR took over operational control of the former Midland main line north of Bristol, as far as Barnt Green, in 1950. This control included making decisions regarding the motive power. One consequence was the use of pannier tanks on the Coaley Junction-Dursley branch, although responsibility for the running sheds (as far north as Bromsgrove) was not transferred until 23rd February 1958. *7th August 1961*

No. 1605 entered traffic 1/11/49 and was allocated to Southall and later to Kidderminster, then Worcester, before transferring to Gloucester (WR) during the w/e 2/11/57. It was withdrawn from Gloucester during the w/e 24/2/62, sold to Cashmore of Newport on 7/5/62 and taken into their yard on 19/5/62. The Mk VI Bentley, registration number NHY 581, first entered traffic carrying Midnight Blue livery (not black as sometimes misquoted) in 1951. Thanks to the loving care bestowed by several owners, it has fared much better than No. 1605 and is still 'clocking up the miles' in 2011. It is often seen, courtesy of current owner Julian Birley, at various heritage railway events.

OPPOSITE PAGE BOTTOM: 'Castle' No. 5087 *Tintern Abbey* heads southward towards Standish with the 4.0pm Cheltenham-Paddington, passing an Up freight bound for Gloucester Eastgate and headed by what appears to be an 0-6-0 working tender first. The WR train commenced its journey from St. James station in Cheltenham and called at Gloucester Central where the direction of travel was reversed. Norman had positioned himself on the overbridge just north of Tuffley Junction, where the former Midland Railway route serving Gloucester Eastgate station parted company with the main line on the right, running to Gloucester Central or directly to Cheltenham via the Cheltenham Loop (or Cheltenham Avoiding Line). *18th April 1961*

The new footsteps on the end of the coach at the rear of the LMR goods train are rather a distraction; one appears to have worked loose already!

'CHALFORD AUTO' VARIETY

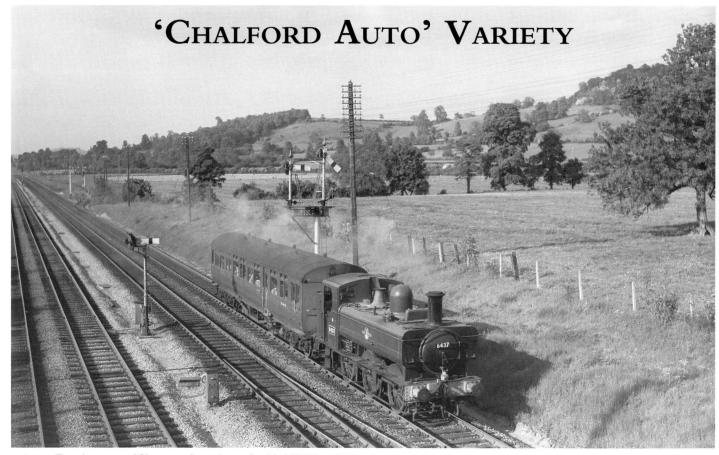

ABOVE: Ten minutes out of Gloucester Central, auto-fitted 0-6-0PT No. 6437 hurries towards Standish Junction with the 6.15pm auto train to Chalford. These services ran 9 miles before a first call at Stonehouse (Burdett Road), then paused at a further intermediate nine stations and wayside halts before reaching Chalford, just 7 miles beyond Stonehouse. *28th May 1960*
Note the differing styles of signals; these were positioned almost opposite the Midland Railway milepost indicating 100 miles as measured from London Road Junction, Derby. The bracket signal on the right is of GWR origin. The unusual design of the signal on the left, with the arm bracketed slightly so as to appear central on the post, was to allow clearance at this otherwise restricted location between the two diverging main lines.

LEFT: Gloucester (Horton Road)-based 0-6-0PT No. 8491 climbing up the bank into Brimscombe station, just behind the photographer. On this occasion Norman failed to record the time – perhaps it was the surprise of seeing this engine on the Chalford service? Delivered new to Swindon in August 1952 from the works of R. Stephenson & Co. (but carrying a Swindon-built boiler), No. 8471 survived in service for just under eleven years, being withdrawn w/e 13/7/63 (from Horton Road) and cut up at Swindon during the 2 w/e 25/1/64. What a waste. *22nd May 1961*
This location puzzled me when I was first sent a low resolution scan from David. However, receipt of the high resolution scan enabled me to enlarge the photograph (up to 400 per cent with little loss of definition). A clue was revealed on the steep hillside in the left background (just to the right of the second telegraph pole). This, I discovered, is Holy Trinity Church near the summit of Brimscombe Hill. So that enabled me to establish the train has just crossed the viaduct between Brimscombe Bridge Halt and Brimscombe West Signal Box.

Standish Junction was a location much favoured by railway photographers in steam days, where the double tracks of the ex-GWR main line to Swindon climb up and swing away to the east from the double track ex-Midland main line which headed south to Bristol, thus marking the southern end of the parallel running which extended southwards for more than 5 miles from Tuffley Junction. Here, 0-4-2T No. 1427 is about to start the climb away from the Midland line, as it passes the signal box at Standish Junction with a well-filled 4.05pm (Sundays) Gloucester-Chalford train, the signalman seen in silhouette standing at the lever frame. The Midland design cabin dated from 1908 and it had just celebrated its 60th birthday when it was closed in October 1968, following simplification of the track layout hereabouts with the lifting of one of the sets of double tracks from Gloucester. Behind the box is the distinctive single arch bridge, which spanned all four tracks and from which Norman had taken the photograph which appears on the previous page, top. *13th September 1959*

This was one of those sections of railway where the designations of each pair of lines serving the two parallel routes were opposites; on the former GWR route the 'Up' direction was towards Swindon whereas 'Up' on the ex-Midland route was towards Gloucester (and onwards to Derby). Passengers on Midland line expresses were often amazed to find themselves overtaken by parallel running auto trains, which regularly attained speeds of 70mph on the fast, level, straight stretch between here and Tuffley!

THE GOLDEN VALLEY, STROUD - 2

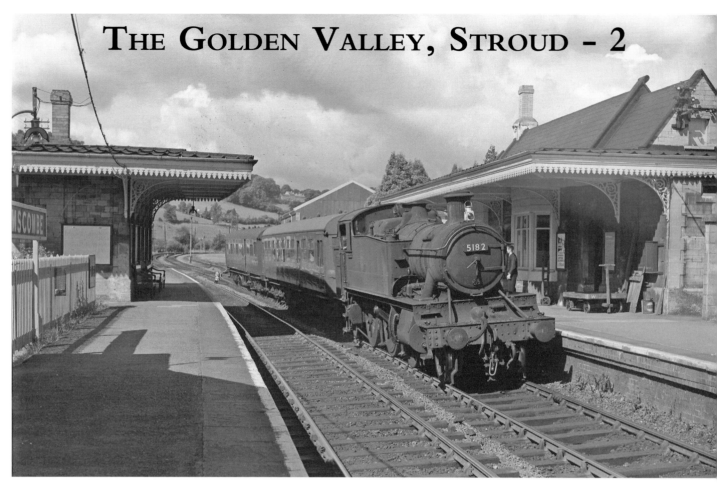

The water tower serving the small locomotive shed at Brimscombe can just be seen to the right of the line, little more than a half-mile away in the distance. The driver of No. 1473 is about to close the regulator for the next call at St. Mary's Crossing Halt less than 2 minutes after setting off from Brimscombe, again with a train consisting of a pair of auto coaches (the loading, one or two coaches, usually depended on the time or day – Saturdays or early morning/late afternoon services being busier). The train, the 10.25am Gloucester-Chalford, is about to pass over the crossing from which the station derives its name. Behind the box and the crossing keeper's cottage, the waters seen are those of the old Thames & Severn Canal, which paralleled much of this section of the line on its climb up the Golden Valley to Sapperton Tunnel. *11th June 1962*
The little signal box and the crossing gates still exist and are now Grade 2 Listed Buildings. The box has long-since ceased controlling any semaphore signals but is still in use for the keeper operating this potentially dangerous crossing, which has restricted visibility for cars and trains in all directions. As a result, the gates are always closed against road traffic, so that permission has to be sought to cross.

OPPOSITE PAGE TOP: 'Large Prairie' No. 5182 might more usually have been found here at Brimscombe on banking or assisting duties for the climb through the Golden Valley. On this occasion, however, the 2-6-2T was deputising for the more usual Collett 'Class 14XX' 0-4-2T (although these photographs show the variety of motive power which might appear) with the 10.08am Gloucester to Chalford. With the time recorded by Norman as 10.48am, the train was running exactly to schedule (Brimscombe depart 10.49am). The delightful Brunellian architecture was not enough to save the station from closure (on 2nd November 1964), nor subsequent demolition and at the site today, there is no evidence whatsover that it ever existed. *7th August 1961*
At the eastern end of the station, looking in the opposite direction to this view, a small single road locomotive shed (a sub shed of Gloucester [WR] mpd) was provided for a pair of 'Large Prairies' which were based here for banking freight trains up the gradient to the summit beyond Sapperton Tunnel or, less frequently, assisting a passenger train from the front.

OPPOSITE PAGE BOTTOM: When Norman and Ivo Peters next visited Brimscombe on a sunny late autumn day in 1961, they happened across No. 6394 attending the clearance of the line following a derailment just to the west of the station. One covered van has already been recovered and loaded. Here, the locomotive is reversing the breakdown train onto the Down line. The jib and exhaust from the steam crane can be seen in the background and note, also, that there is a glimpse of the crane inside the goods shed. *29th October 1961*
Look at the lettering still visible on the wall of the stone-built goods shed; it read 'G W R EXPRESS GOODS TRAIN SERVICES ONE DAY TRANSITS BETWEEN IMPORTANT TOWNS' and was still perfectly legible some 13¾ years after the demise of the Company. Perhaps even more amazingly, however, although this goods shed was demolished shortly after closure of the station, that at Stroud station, now Grade II* Listed and complete with similar lettering, still survives today.

No. 7035 *Ogmore Castle* approaches Chalford station with the 11.45am Cheltenham-Paddington which, after reversal at Gloucester Central, called only at Stroud and Kemble before reaching Swindon. Note the tall Chalford Up Home signal positioned on the 'wrong' side of the line and also fitted with a backing board, both to aid sighting by enginemen. Similarly, the signal seen for the Down line was affixed to a short post so that it could be seen when approaching the footbridge and road overbridge at the west end of the station platform. *11th June 1962*

No. 7035 was one of the final batch of the 'Castle' Class to be constructed at Swindon, released into traffic in August 1950. Following a Light Casual repair at Swindon (19/4/62 to 31/5/62), the 4-6-0 returned to Gloucester (WR) and was withdrawn in June 1965.

RIGHT: The 11.45am Cheltenham-Paddington features again as No. 5071 *Spitfire* heads through Chalford station and attacks the final and steepest 3 miles of the eastbound climb through the extremely picturesque Golden Valley. The perpetrator of the column of steam seen rising behind the train is revealed in the following photograph! *7th August 1961*

BELOW: Two minutes after the passage of the 11.45am from Cheltenham, above, No. 1472 pulls the empty auto train out of the siding behind the Up platform, before propelling the two coaches, via the crossover, onto the Down side to form the 12.45pm back to Gloucester. Despite the bucolic appearance (shades of '*The Titfield Thunderbolt*'!), the 'Chalford Auto' was a well-used and effective service, the cessation of which, after Saturday, 31st October 1964, was met with considerable local regret. *7th August 1961*

The white staining on the chimney and smokebox suggests No. 1472 had suffered a recent and severe bout of priming. Takes you back to those days when soot stains were an occupational hazard of anybody who spent much of their spare time by the lineside or at the end of a station platform! Notice that the small goods yard behind the auto train still contains a couple of wagons, despite the overgrown condition of the sidings.

CHALFORD

ABOVE: The view looking west from the bridge carrying Marley Lane over the railway to the east of Chalford. On a wonderfully clear autumnal morning, the efforts of 2-6-0 No. 6304 are displayed by an impressive exhaust on the climb towards Sapperton with a short permanent way train. Whether this train had been run in connection with reinstating the track following the derailment at Brimscombe (see page 158) was not recorded by Norman. *29th October 1961*
No doubt Norman and Ivo Peters (the latter's Bentley parked adjacent to the lineside and visible above the leading brakevan) heard and saw the exhaust of the 2-6-0 long before the train appeared into view.

LEFT: The trees are still wearing their early summer colours as No. 5017 *The Gloucestershire Regiment 28th 61st* sweeps down the gradients from Sapperton Tunnel with a service bound for Gloucester and Cheltenham. The fireman has time to relax and admire the passing scenery; something not possible here when working hard to maintain boiler pressure on the eastbound run. *11th June 1962*
No. 5017 (see also photograph on the front cover) was originally named St. Donat's Castle when released new into traffic in July 1932 but was renamed on 24th April 1954 in honour of the 'Glorious Glosters' brave endeavours during the Korean War. No. 5017 was withdrawn from service from Gloucester (WR) on 7th September 1962 and sold to Cashmore of Newport in November that same year. One of the nameplates is exhibited at The Soldiers of Gloucestershire Museum, located in the Custom House at Gloucester Docks.

This superb scene was captured near Frampton Mansell as the train – which Norman recorded as the 6.45am (Sundays) Fishguard Harbour to Paddington – was lifted up the 1 in 60 climb nearing Sapperton Tunnel. Both locomotives went unrecorded but doubtless the 2-6-2T was added at Brimscombe and usually would assist as far as Kemble. Only the rather prominent flat-roofed extension to the thatched property detracts from this view. *29th October 1961*

Norman always considered colour photography as very much a 'second best' option. However, this might have proved a rare occasion to have benefited from Norman's occasional use of his 35mm camera which he used to take colour transparencies. The seasonal tints were at their best on this sunny autumn Sunday, when the 'Golden Valley' really was living up to its name. How do I know this? Well, Ivo Peters was on hand to film the same scene in 16mm colour!

KEMBLE

ABOVE: Compared with the bottom picture on the previous page, this elevated position shows a much wider view to include the full length of the platform serving the Cirencester Branch. Slowly gathering speed through the station on the Up main line is 2-6-2T No. 4248 (of Ebbw Junction) hauling a lengthy eastbound freight. This would have been banked from Brimscombe as far as Sapperton Siding Signal Box. There, more likely, the freight would be put into the loop to await a clear line ahead with sufficient time to avoid delay to any following passenger service. East of the summit at Sapperton Siding, the grades towards Purton are generally favourable to Up traffic. *9th June 1961*
As the railhead for Cirencester and Tetbury, Kemble remains a busy station today and it is also now protected by Grade II listing status. A short stub of track also remains to about half way along the Cirencester Branch platform, which is used for the occasional stabling of track machines.

OPPOSITE PAGE TOP: Having made the first scheduled call since departure from Paddington, No. 7035 *Ogmore Castle* sets off from Kemble with the Down 'Cheltenham Spa Express'. *9th June 1962*
Allocated to Gloucester (WR), No. 7035 looks in fine fettle having received what would prove a final Light Intermediate overhaul at Swindon (7/12/61 to 14/2/62). The locomotive is recorded as being withdrawn (from Old Oak Common) on 1/6/64, almost two years to the day after it was photographed here by Norman. Prominent in this evening view is the water tower with a secondary feeder tank carried at a considerable height. Today, the secondary feeder tank has gone but the rest of the water tower survives and is also now Grade II listed. Less prominent, the well known photographer who, over the years, captured Norman on camera far more frequently than was the opposite case! The branch line to Tetbury commenced from the bay platform on the Down side and turned southwards (to the right here) but the course is hidden from view behind the bushes seen beyond the right of where Ivo was standing.

OPPOSITE PAGE BOTTOM: Two days later, the two photographers returned to Kemble, this time to photograph and film the departure of the Up 'Cheltenham Spa Express.' On this occasion, No. 7034 *Ince Castle* is 'doing the honours', here setting off – at 9.04am – for a non-stop journey to arrive at Paddington at 10.35am; a 91 mile run scheduled at an average speed of 60mph. *11th June 1962*
No. 7034 was another '85B' allocation at this time. The sharply curved rails to the right form the junction of the branch line to Cirencester. At this date, the passenger services on both the Cirencester and Tetbury branches were operated by 4-wheeled rail buses which, it appears, Norman elected not to photograph! He and Ivo did return, though, to photograph and film a final steam special, which features later in this book.

ON THE TROUGHS

To be accurate, all but the 4-6-0 and first three coaches of the Up 'Red Dragon' are passing over the water troughs here on the approach to Sodbury Tunnel. Canton's No. 6028 *King George VI* looks in fine fettle having – just moments before – completed taking on water during the scheduled non-stop run from Newport to Paddington. *18th March 1962*

Notice the photographer just visible in the mid-distance. He had the foresight to wear a raincoat and to stand part-way up the side of the cutting. Many years later, I recall him telling me how, despite his precautions, he was still 'hit' by a heavy mist of water such was the strength of the vortex created by the speeding train!

The theme of water troughs proves an opportune 'link' to get us from south Gloucestershire to the borders of 'Oxon & Northants'! On a rather overcast afternoon, No. 6013 *King Henry VIII* picks up water from the troughs just north of Aynho Junction, whilst heading southwards with the 3.35pm Wolverhampton-Paddington. Based at Stafford Road, No. 6013 was destined to be withdrawn just a month later (w/e 9/6/62). The shed plate was already removed when the locomotive was photographed here by Norman. *3rd May 1962*

Taken from the same road overbridge as the previous picture, No. **4951** *Pendeford Hall* – allocated to Reading (WR) – heads towards Aynho Junction with a lengthy Up freight. *3rd May 1962*
This was the scene looking north from the Aynho Road overbridge, with the steeple of Kings Sutton church visible in the left distance. Nowadays the view is interrupted by the passage of the M40 motorway, which sweeps on a curved approach from the south to cross the railway at an oblique angle just beyond the overbridge seen in the distance. These and the following scenes may have been recorded whilst spending a few days in the area during one of the celebrated 'industrial lines' safaris, on which Norman and the Rev'd Alan Newman often joined Ivo Peters, visiting many of the lesser known private railways throughout the country. We hope to feature Norman's photographs from such visits in a later volume.

OXFORD ...

No. 7009 *Athelney Castle* with the Down 'Cathedrals Express' seems to have brought at least one London businessman home for tea! Possibly a 4.45pm departure from London was a little too early to attract such custom in large numbers. I think this train was another example of those which, as referred to earlier in this book, were given a title in 1957 to take advantage of a ruling which permitted the Western Region to re-introduce the chocolate & cream livery to coaching stock – supposedly only for use in 'titled' services. Judging from the background – beyond the locospotters on the far platform – there appeared to be a surfeit of such stock assembled at Oxford that evening. *1st May 1962*

... AND BANBURY

The 'Cambrian Coast Express' calls at Banbury General behind Old Oak's No. 6016 *King Edward V*. Until 1961/2, the 'Cambrian Coast Express' paused for custom at Banbury in the Down direction but at Leamington Spa on the Up service. However, as is evident here, a call at Banbury was introduced into the Up service; this in 1962 and with 15 minutes added to the overall running time. *1st May 1962*

If external appearance was anything by which to judge, No. 6016 was still in excellent condition, yet – on 7/9/62 – would be withdrawn. Banbury station had been rebuilt to the style seen here during the 1950s, the work completed in 1958. The suffix 'General' had been added by BR – but not apparently to the new station lamps – to avoid any possible confusion with the town's other station at Merton Street. The latter, however, closed to passenger traffic in 1961. Standing at the other face of the platform is what I am informed is a Motor Second coach, forming part of a Pressed Steel 3-car suburban DMU.

WORCESTER SHRUB HILL

A busy scene at Worcester Shrub Hill station at 3.10pm, with an 0-6-0PT occupying the nearside platform whilst No. 7009 *Athelney Castle* features again, here seen setting off with the 2.05pm Hereford-Paddington. Notice the once familiar sight on the left of mailbags waiting to loaded – or were they to be collected and taken to the GPO sorting office? The bay platforms at Shrub Hill still handled substantial letter mail and parcels traffic at this date, whilst the station was – and remains – an important cross country junction, although not quite as busy today as in steam days. From here, lines still radiate out south-eastwards to Norton Junction, for the Midland main line south to Cheltenham and Gloucester or east along the ex-GWR route across the Cotswolds to Oxford; west to Malvern and Hereford; and north to Droitwich, where the line splits again for Birmingham via Bromsgrove or Wolverhampton via Kidderminster and Stourbridge. *30th April 1962*

WITHAM & BREWHAM

Back to more accustomed countryside (to this writer!), 0-6-0PT No. 8795 heads down the main line near Witham with the 6.0pm Frome to Yatton service. The main line would be left behind at Witham, from where most of the 'East Somerset/Cheddar Valley' branch line services commenced their journeys to Wells and Yatton, with only a minority extended through to and from Frome. *14th April 1962*
Ivo Peters was well protected from the cold wind – it looked a lovely early evening but the shadows were already lengthening as it was only mid April. Doubtless the gateway on the left – an old occupation crossing – had provided the means of access to the lineside for the two photographers.

Diesel-hydraulic motive power had not yet completely usurped steam on this section of the WR West of England main line by the summer of 1962. No. 4948 *Northwick Hall* (a Swindon allocation and withdrawn 7/9/62) tops the stiff eastbound climb at Brewham with a lengthy freight, possibly originating from Weymouth. The point at which the final 1 in 80 gradient ended is very evident in this view. Those readers of an 'agricultural bent' will observe that the hay crop was now being baled – the traditional hayricks sometimes featuring in the background of Norman's pictures were, generally speaking, already a sign of the past. *7th July 1962*

Under a mackerel sky (a thunderstorm gathering perhaps), No. 5071 *Spitfire* (previously seen on page 161 passing Chalford), with the 5.20pm Westbury to Weymouth semi-fast, has just passed Brewham Signal Box and heads westwards towards Bruton, some 3 to 4 miles distance. With such a lightweight load, the 'Castle' (allocated 82B – St Phillip's Marsh and possibly 'standing in' on a DMU diagram) was hardly exercised by the climb from Witham, which ended adjacent to the signal box seen behind the rear of the train. *15th September 1962*

Apart from this being a rarely featured location, another of my reasons for including this view is because of a friend who – whenever we travel this line – asks me to point out the location of the former Strap Lane Halt. Well, on an HST, invariably we have passed the site before I realise our whereabouts, so here – for that friend – is the location! Had Norman 'pressed the shutter' here pre June-1950, he would have been standing at one end of the wooden Up platform, to which access was gained from the side of the stone overbridge which carries Strap Lane across the railway. No. 5071 entered service in June 1938 as Clifford Castle but was renamed Spitfire in September 1940; the first of a group of a dozen 'Castles' given the names of famous aircraft associated with the Battle of Britain. She was withdrawn from St. Philip's Marsh during the week ending 12th October 1963.

BATH SPA – THE OTHER END!

Another fine summer evening provided Norman this opportunity to photograph Canton-based No. 6935 *Browsholme Hall* in charge of the 5.35pm Salisbury-Cardiff at Bath Spa station. *2nd July 1962* This appears to be the only occasion (when using his quarter-plate camera as against 'experimenting' with 35mm colour transparencies) that Norman took up a position towards the western end of Bath Spa station. The bridge over the River Avon at this end of the station had been widened in 1959, enabling the Up platform to be extended. This followed the removal of a small brick-built stable occupied, certainly into the early-1950s, by 'Prince', the last horse to be used to shunt wagons in and out of the various short 'stub' sidings at both ends of the station.

SWINDON SPECIALS

ABOVE: A Sunday visit to Swindon by No. 6000 *King George VI*, who had returned to 'his' home town with an enthusiast's special from Wolverhampton and Birmingham to Swindon Works. *9th September 1962*

By the time of this visit, most of the 'Kings' had already been withdrawn. All would be gone by the end of the year, with No. 6000 one of the last four to be taken out of service in December 1962. However, after being put aside and languishing in storage at Swindon for several years, 'KGV' was placed on loan with H.P. Bulmer & Co., cider makers of Hereford, who financed restoration to main line running condition. As such, in 1971 the locomotive became the first steam engine to break the BR ban that had been in place since 1969. The Down side of the station at Swindon (Swindon Junction until closure of the 'Town' station in 1961) was later demolished in the early 1970s, as part of the redevelopment which included a multi-story office block. In 2003, an additional platform was constructed on the Down side, such had been the proliferation of passenger traffic by rail since the latter years of the 20th century.

RIGHT: No. 6874 *Haughton Grange* looks resplendent in a new coat of green livery, with black & orange lining and a freshly painted 3,500 gallon tender. This locomotive proved to be amongst the last of the class to be built, in 1939, because the outbreak of hostilities interrupted further construction and post-war, this was destined never to be resumed. No. 6874 had just received a final General Repair following a few months allocated to Penzance (83G). On return to the West Country, just days after being photographed here by Norman, the allocation was to Laira. *24th June 1962*

Following subsequent reallocations, to Didcot on 7/9/1962 and Oxford w/e 7/10/63, No. 6874 was withdrawn from this latter shed on 10/9/65. Sold to Cashmore of Newport on 21/10/65, the locomotive was recorded as taken into their yard on 13/1/66.

Following the harshest winter the West Country had experienced since 1946/7, Norman (in company with Ivo Peters) paid another visit to Swindon on a *very* wet Sunday in March 1963. Both photographers had been undeterred by drifts of several feet of snow on the Mendips just a few weeks earlier, so some heavy rainfall was of little consequence! This was an opportunity just too good to miss, with two famous locomotives resting side by side and this shot was achieved by standing just inside the open-fronted running shed. By this date, both locomotives had been scheduled by BR for preservation: ex-L&NER 'A4' Class 'Pacific' No. 60022 *Mallard*, which had arrived with a special from Southampton, keeping company with No. 6000 *King George V*. *17th March 1963*
Notice the Class '52' diesel-hydraulic tucked behind the 'King'. That's the closest we get in this book to seeing a 'Western'!

This Sunday special provided a final opportunity to travel behind a 'King' Class locomotive in BR service. No. 6018 *King Henry VI* – having just arrived – is about to draw the train forward before setting back onto the Up main line to gain access to a siding serving the Works. In the background is Rodbourne Lane Signal Box, located about a half mile west of Swindon station whilst, extreme right, is the tower of St. Marks, the church provided by subscription by the GWR and dedicated in 1845. *28th April 1963*
No. 6018 had been withdrawn from Old Oak Common and sent to Swindon the previous December. However, following some repairs the locomotive was specially reinstated to Birmingham (Tyseley w/e 27/4/63) to work this trip to Swindon and back. For a few days prior to the special, No. 6018 was reported to be working local trains between Snow Hill and Leamington Spa. The special ran via Leamington and the Greenford Loop and included a visit to Slough mpd. Note the smokebox numberplate and shedplate had been removed; the former substituted with the number painted 'Great Western' style on the front buffer beam. The 'King' was withdrawn (again) the day following the SLS tour and cut up at Swindon during the week ending 21st September 1963.

MORETON-IN-MARSH

Two hours after departure from London, No. 7031 *Cromwell's Castle* pulls away from Moreton-in-Marsh with the 1.15pm Paddington to Hereford. The station stands just to the other side of the overbridge which carries the Fosseway (A429) and – until 1960 – had been the junction for a branch line to Shipston-on-Stour (freight only from 1929) which, itself originated as part of the horse-drawn Stratford & Moreton Tramway. *15th April 1963*

No. 7031, released from Swindon Works in June 1950, spent most of a short working life allocated in the West Country. However, she was transferred to Worcester w/e 17/7/62 from where she was withdrawn w/e 13/7/63, four months after being photographed here by Norman. BR singled much of the route between Norton Junction, near Worcester, and Yarnton Junction, near Oxford, in the early 1970s – as an economy measure. However, as these words were being written in autumn 2011, a project to redouble much of it again was completed, including returning two tracks to this section heading north from Moreton-in-Marsh. Despite this work, however, the signal box at the station, which dates from circa 1884, has been retained to operate the local semaphore signals.

A 'WESTERNISED' S&D

ABOVE: Having a boiler derived from the GWR No. 2 type, Swindon–built BR 'Standard' Class '3' 2-6-T No. 82001 runs along a section of track of the S&D which, originally, had been laid as mixed gauge (well there's three good justifications to include the S&D in this book!). In lined green livery, No. 82001 heads north near Wyke Champflower, between Cole and Evercreech Junction, with the 4.05pm Templecombe to Highbridge local. Note the figure just to the right of the nearest telegraph pole – Ivo Peters was photographing his favourite line ahead of what would prove the final summer of through holiday traffic. Although the WR had been in control of motive power matters at all S&D sheds since 1958, the line still retained its own headlamp codes – this despite a 'missive' in 1958 to conform to the standard codes! *14th April 1962 This locomotive came to Templecombe mpd from Chester (LMR), first on loan 12/4/61, then allocated on 23rd of the same month, where it remained until transferred to Hereford during w/e 11/8/62. After several more allocations and a period in storage, the engine moved to Bath Green Park during w/e 27/11/65, only to be withdrawn on 31/12/65. No. 82001 was sold to Cashmore of Newport 11/2/66 and taken into their yard 5/4/66.*

LEFT: The Collett 0-6-0s had become so embedded in the motive power used on the S&D by 1962 that they were even used for enthusiast's specials – now that really was 'rubbing salt into the wound' of some diehards! No. 3210 passes Pylle Halt, the first station reached from Evercreech Junction on the original S&D main line to Burnham. By this date, Pylle Halt had all but sunk into oblivion; even so the WR authorised the external redecoration of both station and signal box, the latter reduced to the status of a ground frame as long ago as 1911. *30th September 1962 No. 3210 had been transferred to Templecombe from 11/10/60 and remained there until withdrawn on 13/11/64. It was sold 12/1/65 to Cashmore of Newport and taken into their yard on 1/4/65. Despite my comment above, I have it on the authority of one ex-Templecombe footplateman that the Collett 0-6-0s were given the 'thumbs up' by at least some of those driving and firing on the S&D!*

This special (*and opposite below*) was 'The Somerset & Dorset Rail Tour', a Sunday outing organised by the Locomotive Club of Great Britain. In addition to a run up the main line behind more traditional S&D motive power, the itinerary included a trip along the branch from Evercreech Junction to Highbridge and back. Here, No. 3210 sets off after a pause at Glastonbury, originally the headquarters of the S&DR and the western end of the original broad gauge Somerset Central Railway from Highbridge Wharf, which opened in 1854. *30th September 1962* Notice the headcode – conformity at last – but perhaps only for this return run over the branch! Note also the famous landmark, Glastonbury Tor, visible on the distant skyline. The young lad is attempting to 'race the train' – I wonder if he is still living locally at the time this book is first published half a century later?

SOMERSET BYWAYS

Wells (Tucker Street) station remained, until early September 1963, as the last to serve the smallest city in England, which once could boast three stations all within a radius of a few hundred yards. Here, however, is a scene on the last day of passenger traffic over the Yatton to Witham line, as Ivatt 2-6-2T No. 41245 (a Bristol, Barrow Road allocation) comes to rest with a Saturdays only Cheddar Valley service from Yatton. This train terminated here, to form a return working to Yatton, rather than running through to Witham. The signalman returns to his box with the single line token for the section from Cheddar. Unlike many other closures during the early 1960s, this 'last day' did not appear to generate much interest amongst the good folk of Wells, judging from the near deserted appearance here at Tucker Street. Perhaps they all turned out later in the day. *7th September 1963*

Wells was the point where two separate branch lines, the Cheddar Valley line from Yatton and the East Somerset line from Witham met 'end-on' to create the through route between Yatton and Witham. This union was achieved only by passing over a few chains of the S&D branch from Glastonbury to Wells – hence the origins of the three stations! (see The East Somerset & Cheddar Valley Railways *by Richard Harman, Lightmoor Press 2009)*

A remarkably clean Collett 0-6-0, No. 3218, arrives at Shepton Mallet (High Street) with the last eastbound train, the 2.45pm Yatton to Witham, again on the final day of passenger traffic. In contrast, rather scruffy looking BR 'Standard' Class '3' 2-6-2T No. 82037 waits to leave with a westbound train; the event watched by a couple of young lads and captured on camera by enthusiasts in the front coach of No. 3218's train.

As the suffix to the name suggests, the 'East Somerset' station at Shepton Mallet was centrally placed – having been sited at the south end of the High Street. The S&D station at Charlton Road, however, was less conveniently positioned, on the eastern edge of a town perhaps best known as the home of 'Babycham', a sparking Perry, the first alcoholic drink to be advertised on television in the British Isles.

Barrow Road's 0-6-0PT No. 4699 passes the fixed Up Distant signal on the approach to Clutton, with the 4.25pm coal train from Old Mills to Bristol East Depot. The load was in all probability destined for the power station at Portishead. *27th September 1963*

A delightful scene from the 'North Somerset line' which linked Frome – via Radstock and Pensford – to North Somerset Junction, Bristol. Passenger services to and from Temple Meads had been withdrawn at the start of November 1959 but freight traffic, mostly minerals and coal, kept this section of the line west of Radstock open until severe flood damage in July 1968 led to a decision to close this major part of the route and thereafter take out coal from the Radstock area via Frome. A few miles at the eastern (Frome) end of the branch remain open for the stone traffic generated from the large quarry at Whatley, whilst with the rails between Frome and Radstock still largely intact, albeit in need of relaying, the North Somerset Railway Company is promoting the reopening of the line between these two towns to passenger traffic. That will not include the northern half of the line on which No. 4699 is seen here, along which the viaduct at Pensford is now the largest surviving structure.

The 'Mendip Rail Tour', an enthusiast's special organised by the Home Counties Railway Society, included a trip along the Yatton to Witham branch line. Here 2-6-2T's No's 4103 and 6148 head down the main line between Bristol and Yatton, prior to gaining the branch. The weather was far from ideal for photography. *6th October 1963*
The 'Mendip Rail Tour' commenced from London and ran to Bristol behind LMR No 45552 Silver Jubilee. *The two 'Large Prairie' tanks took over to continue the special to Westbury via the Cheddar Valley and East Somerset lines. The return from Westbury to London was made via Salisbury and the SR main line to Waterloo.*

RAIL TOURS

Still in Somerset, an Ian Allan Rail Tour turns off the main line at Norton Fitzwarren and heads for Barnstaple. Motive power from Paddington as far as Taunton (via Newbury and Devizes) had been ex-L&NER Class 'A3' 'Pacific' No. 4472 *Flying Scotsman*. The train, composed of ten Pullman coaches, was taken over at Taunton by this pair of ex-GWR 'Moguls' – No's 7317 and 7332 – the external appearance of which was rather an embarrassment in comparison with the restored and privately owned No. 4472. The two 2-6-0s took the special forward to Barnstaple and Ilfracombe, then back to Exeter Central, where *Flying Scotsman* was waiting to return the tour to London. *19th October 1963*
As the captions in this book were finalised, the first permanent way trains have made their way along the track relaid by the West Somerset Railway Association along the first half mile or so of the former Barnstaple Branch line, to form a part of the 'Norton triangle' created for the WSR. Now nearing total completion, this project will allow locomotives, stock and even complete trains to be turned, a truly remarkable achievement.

Yeovil 'Bunk'

ABOVE: The shuttle service linking Yeovil Town station with Yeovil Junction, on the SR Salisbury-Exeter main line, was for many years the domain of former L&SWR Class 'M7' 0-4-4Ts. Towards the end of March 1963, these stalwarts gave way to ex-GWR 0-6-0PTs. Then, in October 1963, at least two Collett 0-4-2Ts were introduced to the service. Here, No. 1442 sets off from the Town station on the 1¾mile journey to the Junction, which occupied no more than 5 minutes. *3rd November 1963*

BELOW: At the very end of 1964, two AC Car's 46 seat rail buses were transferred to Yeovil to take over the service. However, this was not the end of the line for the Collett 0-4-2Ts; No's 1442 and 1450 were transferred to Exmouth Junction and worked the Seaton Branch during a temporary shortage of DMUs! Here they are at Axminster, where they paused for water whilst making their way to Exmouth Junction which was in the control of the Western Region by this date. The lighting was poor but a pair of these engines was, surely, a unique sight heading down the former L&SWR main line towards Exeter. *7th February 1965 Both of the 0-4-2Ts were withdrawn from Exmouth Junction on 7/5/65; No. 1442 was sold to Sir John Amery/Tiverton Transport Museum on 25/6/65 and No. 1450 to the GWS just four days later.*

1964 LINESIDE VISITS

Norman had come with Ivo Peters to the lineside at Charlbury troughs (between Charlbury and Ashcott-under-Wychwood) to photograph an Oxford University Railway Society Special train. Ivo's photograph and film of that event have appeared before, so it was fortuitous that, whilst waiting for the special, this local ambled past. Norman recorded the time as 1.55pm but gave no indication as to the train service. *16th May 1964*
This section of the Cotswolds line was also singled in the 1970s but, in 2011, has seen its second track reinstated. The improvements, to provide extra capacity on this important cross-country route, have included the reinstatement of the second platforms at both Charlbury and Ascott-under-Wychwood stations. The station building at Charlbury is a remarkable survivor, built of wood in the Italianate style favoured by Brunel, it is Grade II listed, along with its GWR nameboard.

THE HSBT PROJECT

Those readers who have seen a copy of *Great Western Steam 1934-1949* may recall our placing on record our thanks to the HSBT Project. Anybody wishing to quote or source data regarding the withdrawal and scrapping of steam locomotives will be only too aware of just how frequently they have to resort to 'secondary sources' for such information. As a consequence – and here we quote from *The Railway Magazine*, November 2009 – '*For more than 20 years, book authors and magazine writers have unwittingly perpetuated errors with regard to the withdrawal and scrapping of many BR steam locomotives*'. However, now a major project is underway to set the record straight as to what really happened to steam. Known as 'The HSBT Project', this is researching and will publish the definitive record, as gathered only from primary sources, including official railway records and those of private sector scrapyards. This represents a major challenge and a time-consuming task. However, we are extremely pleased to be able to state that our own book – as with the earlier GWR volume – has benefited from the creation of The HSBT Project. So our thanks go again to the Project and, in particular, to Roger Butcher (the member of the project with primary responsibility for Western Region data) who has, wherever possible, checked the withdrawal and/or scrapping dates quoted by Mike in his captions. Much help has also been given regarding allocations and dates of visits by locomotives to Swindon Works for repair. (By the way, in case you are wondering, 'HSBT' is an acronym formed of the initials of the surnames of each of the four people responsible for the Project!)

No. 6849 *Walton Grange* turns away southwards from the WR West of England direct line at Castle Cary with the 11.10am (SO) Wolverhampton to Weymouth train. After a journey time of 5¼ hrs since departure from Wolverhampton (Low Level), this train would continue from Castle Cary with calls made at Yeovil (Pen Mill), Maiden Newton (for the Bridport Branch) and Dorchester West, to reach Weymouth in about another 70 minutes. *25th July 1964*

Notice the unusual style of signal box; a war-time replacement following destruction of the existing box by an air raid presumably to 'take out' this rural yet strategic railway junction. The former 'Wilts, Somerset & Weymouth' line has long since been singled between here and Dorchester. Like all of the once popular 'Grange' Class, No. 6849 did not survive into the 'preservation era'. However, in 1998, the '6880 Society' was formed with the sole intention of recreating a new locomotive of this class. The Society (a registered charity) is based on the Llangollen Railway in Denbighshire.

0-4-2T
SPECIALS

The Collett '48XX' 0-4-2Ts became a popular choice of motive power on specials which visited various WR branch lines around Wiltshire, Somerset and Gloucester in the mid-1960s. Sadly, this was often associated with the running of 'last day' or similar events to mark the demise of such lines but explains why Norman frequently photographed examples of these fine little ex-GWR locos around this time.

ABOVE: Collett 0-4-2T No. 1472 was the motive power used for a special on Sunday, 5th April 1964, organised by the Gloucestershire Railway Society. This visited both the Tetbury and Cirencester branch lines. Tetbury was the terminus of the 7¼ mile single line branch from Kemble and had been closed to all public services on the previous day. Here, the tour sets off on the return run from the attractive single platform terminus at Tetbury, just glimpsed in the right background.

RIGHT: Ivo Peters' driving skills enabled him and Norman to get ahead of the train to photograph and film the return run from Tetbury. The 0-4-2T and its train of two auto trailers are here seen on the embankment near Culkerton station.
Remarkably, whilst Tetbury and Culkerton stations have long since been demolished, the goods sheds at both still survive at the time of writing.

LEFT: Another piece of speedy driving brought the two photographers back to Kemble station in time to witness the Special transferring to the sharply curved platform line which served as the start of the 4¼ mile branch line to Cirencester; a town which was set to lose the second of its two stations (the other – see page 152 – having been located on the M&SWJR line). This branch closed on the day of the visit by the Special train, the last public service running later in the day.
Another of Norman's photographs of the Special, leaving Cirencester for the return journey, appears on the rear cover of this book. Both branch lines had, since 1959, been operated using Swindon based lightweight diesel rail buses, at which time four low level additional halts (two on each branch) had been provided in an attempt to reduce operating costs and attract more passengers.

No. 1444 heads past Hawkeridge Junction, on the approach to Westbury on the line from Trowbridge, with a special organised by the Great Western Society. Commencing from Swindon, the tour visited the Calne Branch before continuing to Westbury and a visit to the locomotive depot. Then a return was made via Bath, Bristol and the Badminton route back to Swindon. The cost for this circular tour, which traversed some very pleasant countryside, was 35 shillings (£1.75p). *20th September 1964*

The line seen diverging to the right behind the signal box was installed during the Second World War – connecting with the main line to Reading at Heywood Road Junction. It became known as Westbury East Chord and remains in use to the present day, providing a useful diversionary (if somewhat circuitous) route between Bath and Reading. A 'certainty' for inclusion, as this location is but a couple of miles from where these captions have been 'word processed' and still witnessing the passage of steam specials in 2012.

STEAM SPECIALS

This Special was organised by the Stevenson Locomotive Society (Midland Area) and ran from Birmingham, via the Shrewsbury Avoiding Curve, to Hereford and on to Severn Tunnel Junction. Shed visits were planned at both Hereford and Severn Tunnel Junction. On the next stage of the run, No. 4079 *Pendennis Castle* is seen emerging from the eastern end of the Severn Tunnel, en route to Swindon, where visits to the Works Yard and Running Shed were planned. The train returned to Birmingham via Oxford. *26th April 1964*

No. 7022 *Hereford Castle* was, I understand, stationed here as a 'stand-by' engine in conjunction with the running of the final leg (Bristol-Paddington) of an Ian Allan rail tour. This tour had been arranged to celebrate the sixtieth anniversary of the record speed (circa 102½mph) attained by *City of Truro* whilst descending Wellington bank. Happily, No. 7022 complete with a wooden replica number plate on the smokebox, was not required – the selected 'Castle' for this leg, No. 5054, passing through Swindon at 80 mph. The 'Castle' Class was going out in a blaze of glory but the real drama had occurred earlier in the day when No. 4079 *Pendennis Castle* dropped some of her firebars near Lavington! Having just reached 96mph on the outward run of the special to Plymouth when the incident occurred, the locomotive had to be nursed to Westbury and taken off the train. *9th May 1964*

'The North & West Limited Rail Tour' was organised by the LCGB, running from London to Swindon for a visit of the Works yard and running shed. No. 7029 *Clun Castle* took over at Swindon and is seen emerging, 'wrong line', (the consequence of Sunday engineering works) from Sodbury Tunnel on the next leg, via the Badminton line and the Severn Tunnel, to Hereford. From there, the tour travelled via the avoiding line at Shrewsbury to Wolverhampton and back to London. *21st June 1964*
Part of the village of Old Sodbury lies over this end of the tunnel, whilst beyond, on the skyline, can be seen the castellated tower of the most westerly of the seven access shafts, all of which were retained to provide ventilation for the 4,444yd tunnel.

'S&D Tour'

The 'Wessex Downsman' was another rail tour organised by the LCGB. Commencing at Waterloo, the special stopped at Reading where No. 6963 *Throwley Hall* took over for the run, via Devizes, to Bath and Bristol. The train is here passing Bathampton *en route* to Temple Meads. There the direction reversed, returning to Bath but via the former Midland Railway line behind 0-6-0 Class '4F' No. 44466 to Green Park station. Next followed another reverse of direction and a run down the full length of the S&D main line to Bournemouth, before the return – via Southampton – to Waterloo. *4th April 1965*
This itinerary proved so popular that, a month later, on 2nd May 1965, the LCGB ran a repeat tour which features in our companion album The Somerset & Dorset Railway 1935-1966. *Notice the train is composed of Bulleid stock which was painted in green livery. The year of this photograph, 1965, was when BR introduced the new 'blue & light cream' corporate livery but you may be pleased to learn that within these pages we are spared such a sight (even in monochrome!).*

CLUN CASTLE

ABOVE: No. 7029 *Clun Castle* draws some admiring glances on arrival at Swindon with 'The Western Venturer', a rail tour from Paddington which continued to Bath, then via Dr Day's Bridge Junction (Bristol) and Stoke Gifford to join the Midland main line to Gloucester. From Engine Shed Junction, Gloucester, the special continued behind No. 6848 *Toddington Grange* over the Stratford-on-Avon line to Birmingham and then south again to Worcester. At Shrub Hill station, No. 7029 was waiting to take over once more for the return to London via Oxford and Reading. *6th February 1965*

RIGHT: This SLS special comprised a 450 mile round trip from Birmingham, which travelled via Reading and Basingstoke to Salisbury behind Bulleid 'Light Pacific' No. 34051 *Winston Churchill*. At Salisbury, the special was taken over by No. 35017 *Belgian Marine* for the continuation to Exeter and back to Westbury. There, the 'Merchant Navy' was replaced by No. 7029 for the journey across to Bristol and home to Birmingham. It was 6.15pm when Norman photographed the train just to the west of Bath, following its passage through Twerton Tunnel. *23rd May 1965*

No. 7029 remains today as one of the locomotives based at Tyseley, the home of the Birmingham Railway Museum Trust where, as at autumn 2011, it is undergoing another major overhaul. In the past forty plus years since preservation, the 4-6-0 has travelled widely on main line excursions, attended many Open Days and visited heritage railways around the country. In 1985, *Clun Castle* played a prominent role in the Great Western Railway 150th Anniversary celebrations, hauling main line trains to Cornwall and South Wales.

PRIVATE OWNERSHIP

HANDOVER OF NO. 4079

ABOVE: Norman's last visit to Swindon Works was undertaken in the company of Ivo Peters, who had brought along his cine camera to film this event. No. 4079 *Pendennis Castle* was officially withdrawn on 11/5/1964 and sold by BR on 16/11/64. After an overhaul at Swindon Works, which included a repaint in GWR livery, No. 4079 was officially handed over to its new owner. Still very much representing the 'Castle' Class 'as built', this 4-6-0 has proved one of the most popular examples of the products of Swindon Works to pass into what is known today as the 'railway heritage' business but, in 1965, was still an emerging 'steam railway preservation movement'. *11th April 1965*

Prior to releasing a video which included the film of this event (see The Ivo Peters Collection – Volume Fifteen*), extensive enquiries were made to establish the names of each of the people seen in the line-up above. They are (l. to r.); A.A.W. Loveday, Assistant Works Manager; Michael Higson; Mrs Higson; R.F. Hanks, Chairman of BR Western Area Board; The Mayor of Swindon, Mr M. Webb;. F.W. Hawksworth, former CME of the GWR; J. (Jock) Scott, Chief Works Manager. The two men wearing the light coloured overcoats (standing immediately in front of the locomotive's nameplate) are Tom Matthewson-Dick, Assistant General Manager Technical at Paddington, and J.W. Innis, Chief Draftsman, C&W. At the near end is H.W. Mear. Also present (but hidden from view from this angle and standing between Messrs Matthewson-Dick and Innis) was A.W.J. Dymond, Chief Stores Manager, Swindon. The name of the man in the left background, going about his work, went unrecorded! No. 4079 was bought by Mike Higson through the Great Western Society and to whom the sale was invoiced; the negotiations having been undertaken by Ken Williams, who was Chairman of the GWS at that time. Following the sale and a short stay based at Southall, No. 4079 was moved, in turn, to the disused fitting shop at Didcot mpd, to Market Overton and to Steamtown (Carnforth), during which period ownership changed hands a couple of times. In 1977, the engine was sold to Hammersley Iron in Australia and exported later that year. However, in 2000 it was offered free of charge to the GWS and after the substantial shipping and movement costs had been raised,* Pendennis Castle *returned to England and the headquarters of the Great Western Society at the Didcot Railway Centre.*

OPPOSITE PAGE TOP: Privately owned No. 4555 and No. 1420 have arrived back at Worcester Shrub Hill after hauling a special organised by the SLS (Midland Area). This commenced at Birmingham Snow Hill and ran to Worcester via Kidderminster behind ex-L&NER Class 'K4' No. 6442 *The Great Marquis*. At Worcester, the two ex-GWR locomotives took over for the run, via Stourport-on-Severn and Bewdley, to Alveley Colliery (*see below*). The two tank engines then returned the special via Kidderminster to Birmingham, before heading the train back to Worcester where they were photographed here by Norman. *Goodness! Norman has allowed the corner of (is it?) a Brush Type 4 to creep into the edge of the frame – but only as far as necessary to balance his shot!*

OPPOSITE PAGE BOTTOM: Earlier in the day, No. 1420 paused whilst running round the special train at Alveley Colliery sidings on the Severn Valley line. This was a tour which enabled the fledgling SVR Association, formed at Kidderminster just 2½ months earlier, to bring itself to the attention of around 300 passengers, who travelled on the special. Today, the SVR is amongst the finest (many would argue the finest) of this country's heritage railways. *Sunday 19th September 1965 Alveley Colliery was closed by the NCB during January 1963, an event which would lead to the SVR extending its Bridgnorth-Hampton Loade train services southwards, first to Highley from 12th April 1974, then – from 18th May 1974 – to Bewdley. No. 4555 was withdrawn from Laira during the week ending 23rd November 1963 and sold 19th May 1964. No. 1420 had been withdrawn from Gloucester (Western Region) during the week ending 31st October 1964 and sold on 7th April 1965. Both sales were to Pat Whitehouse, who had arranged the repair and the restoration of the livery as seen above.*

No. 4079 *Pendennis Castle* back out 'on the road' in all her glory. This was the 'Ian Allan Rail Tour' from Paddington to Worcester, out via Gloucester and return via Gloucester and Swindon. After departure from Gloucester, followed by the climb of Sapperton Bank and the passage of Sapperton Tunnel, No. 4079 accelerated rapidly on the favourable gradients towards Kemble and Purton. Cecil J Allen (*Railway World* – Feb. 66) reported that, from a speed of around 30mph on passing Sapperton Sidings Signal Box (seen above in the left background), No. 4079 'went like the wind' covering the next 13 miles or so to Purton at an average of **83.4mph**. *Sunday 8th August 1965 (14.50hrs)*

Thirty-one years before taking this photograph, Norman Lockett had captured an image of the same locomotive climbing Hemerdon Incline. The date, 12th June 1934, was one of Norman's first lineside visits with a camera (see page 17 of Great Western Steam 1934-1949). At that time, the locomotive – only the seventh member of the class to be built – had already made its 'claim to fame' by taking part, in May 1925, in the locomotive exchange between the L&NER and the GWR. Later that year, the GWR sent this locomotive to the second Wembley Exhibition to sit alongside L&NER Class 'A3' 'Pacific' Flying Scotsman. This book is published in 2011 and, hopefully in the not too distant future, No. 4079 will emerge resplendent yet again, following a lengthy and very extensive overhaul by the Great Western Society.